a mother's tears

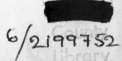

a mother's tears

A story of stillbirth and life

NICOLE WYBORN

First published in 2010 by Jane Curry Publishing
(Wentworth Concepts Pty Ltd)
PO Box 780 Edgecliff NSW 2027

Web: www.janecurrypublishing.com.au

National Library of Australia
Cataloguing-in-Publication data:
    Wyborn, Nicole.
    A mother's tears : a story of stillbirth and life.
    1st edition.
    ISBN 9780980721270
    Stillbirth-Psychological aspects.
    Miscarriage-Psychological aspects.
    Bereavement.
    Childbirth.
    155.937

Design: Cheryl Collins Design
Printed in Australia by McPherson's Printing Group

For Benjamin

'An angel in the book of life wrote down my baby's birth,
Then quietly whispered as he closed the book,
"too beautiful for earth".'

Author Unknown

contents

foreword

When the subject of infant death is discussed by health professionals, you will hear words such as products of conception, obstetric history, perinatal death, chorioamnionitis, stillbirth, placental insufficiencies, autopsy, polyamnios, anticardiopilin antibodies, statistics etc – medical jargon devoid of emotion and empathy.

When you listen to a bereaved parent, you will hear words such as anger, guilt, anguish, despair, devastation, living a nightmare, surreal, being in a daze, pain and longing – words that are so descriptive and yet are insufficient and inadequate to convey the depth of those feelings. The pain of losing a child is something that lives with you forever – you don't 'get over it' – you just live through it. Such is the continuum of life.

A Mother's Tears gives insight into the world of midwifery from a clinical perspective, but also from a very personal perspective as Nicole Wyborn describes her journey through the loss of three babies or, clinically speaking, two miscarriages and one neonatal death. The reality of the pain of three dreams unfulfilled, three lives unlived is poignant to readers whether they be bereaved parents, health professionals or friends and family of those suffering the loss.

Infant mortality often remains a taboo subject in our society despite the fact that long gone are the days where women had their precious babies taken from them and buried without them even having the chance to hold them. Ongoing work, education, and support by SIDS and Kids and the Australian New Zealand Stillbirth Alliance (ANZSA) to health professionals is providing them with the skills and information to provide optimum care to families when they experience such a tragic loss.

A Mother's Tears also encapsulates and provides insight into the anxieties that arise when families go on to have a child following miscarriage or stillbirth. Often fears become intertwined with excitement. There is also the battle between the acknowledgement that this next baby's birth is wonderful, and the fact that it is also tinged with sadness, as memories of the previous experience raise their head. These families understand better than anyone that most parents' worst nightmare, can, and has previously, become a sad reality.

Nicole provides hope to bereaved families and shows them that they WILL survive this tragic event. Health professionals will also gain a valuable insight, which will inform their ability to provide optimum care for bereaved families by reading Nicole's journey – *A Mother's Tears*.

Sue-Ellen Robertson

Sue-Ellen Robertson is the CEO of SIDS and Kids Hunter Region. She trained as a registered nurse in the 1980s in a small country town. During her training several families she knew or cared for experienced the death of their baby or young child during pregnancy, birth and infancy. These experiences however did not prepare her for the devastation she felt when her second son died suddenly and unexpectedly in 1990. She became involved with SIDS and Kids, developing an interest in the new education programs aimed at reducing the incidence of SIDS. A new passion is to see a risk reduction campaign to lower the incidence of unexplained stillbirth in Australia. Sue-Ellen has worked closely with many bereaved parents over the years and is humbled by newly bereaved families allowing her to walk beside them on their journey of grief. She has represented SIDS and Kids regarding bereavement support and education programs to families, health professionals and researchers nationally and internationally.

preface

I always said my child-bearing years were from thirty to thirty-five. In that time we, my husband Kane and I, had planned to have three children. Having control and a five year plan in our life was what secured our home, university degrees and strong careers. If someone told me that in order to complete our family we would have two miscarriages and a stillbirth I would have laughed in disbelief. Having now experienced this we wouldn't have it any other way, all of our children are a blessing. This is my story about the agony and ecstasy of having a family and moving forward through grief.

introduction

Being a midwife is a privilege. I didn't understand just how much of a privilege at the tender age of twenty-three when I completed my training. Looking back, I was totally unaware of the impact I had on women and their families. The blessing I find in midwifery is that I get to care for women who are happy the majority of the time, in comparison to my previous nursing experience which was in a neurological setting. In the neurological ward there were very few happy cases and I couldn't bear one more tragic situation in which people were given the terrible news that they were going to die a slow and painful death from motor neurone disease or inoperable brain cancer. I had to get out after working there for only one year, when going to the pub after a night shift was the only way to get some sleep. I still recall some of the patients I cared for vividly as their situations were so cruel and inhumane. I thought that in midwifery I would find the opposite of death: life and birth. What could be happier than that, I thought, caring for women that are well, no more having to give bad news and I promptly completed my application for the course and was successful. I left the busy city hospital for the coast.

The course in midwifery was intense; we were doing a two year program in one year which meant giving up full time work for six months. We did rotations through all areas of caring for pregnant women including the antenatal clinic, the birthing suite, the postnatal and special care nursery, and we had to pass competencies and exams in these areas to qualify as a midwife. I can still recall the first birth I witnessed during the birthing suite rotation. I wonder what the senior midwife thought of me gripping her arm trying to stop myself from passing out whilst the woman giving birth appeared to be murdered with pain from pushing out her screaming baby. I wondered what had I got myself into! Thankfully, trainee midwives had to witness five births before taking an active role themselves. By the time I reached this stage my confidence had grown and I was able to put on a pair of gloves and cradle my hand around the baby's head whilst the mother screamed uncontrollably, didn't do as she was instructed, and pushed her baby out shoulders and all. She had one of the worst tears I have seen to this day. Supervising the first birth

I assisted was a team of five doctors. I felt in pain myself for this woman and so embarrassed that I couldn't do more to control the situation. In summary, I felt like a dickhead and wondered how I was going to finish the course.

Thank God the birthing suite wasn't the only rotation I had to do. I loved all the other aspects of midwifery; assisting and educating women in clinics and teaching women about bathing and breastfeeding was a joy. I particularly loved working in the special care nursery; feeding and caring for the premature babies, watching them grow and go home. I have some great memories of that time. Although I was confident in these areas, my birthing suite rotation remained unmastered.

During my time in the birthing suite as a trainee midwife I was asked to look after a lady having a baby that had died *in utero* and I was assisted by the senior midwife who delivered the first birth I saw. I can still recall her saying, 'You have to do this at some stage.' It made me realise that although the majority of pregnant women experience the happiest times of their lives, some women also experience the worst. This was a hard lesson to learn at twenty-three, especially when I had no intention of having children for many years. We gave the lady the same care as we did other women, but what we did after the birth was so different. I felt so much sadness for this woman and tried to make her situation as tolerable as possible by dressing her beautiful daughter in pretty, pink knitted clothes, petite booties and bonnet and wrapping her in laced trimmed sheets. I realised I could not begin to understand what she was going through and couldn't try, but I did all I could to make everything as bearable as possible, and that meant giving something to her that she would remember her little girl by. Until I experienced stillbirth myself I had no idea of the pain these women and families go through. No one can who hasn't been there. It is the most devastating thing that can happen to a woman.

Fortunately with time and experience I improved in the birthing suite rotation and I passed all aspects of my training. One of my final deliveries in my training days was a lady labouring in the bath and she stayed there until it was time to birth. The room was so calm and serene; she birthed her baby her way and marked the end of my time in the birthing suite.

It was after I moved to the coast that I met my husband, Kane. Initially I had to leave full time work for my midwifery course and I had moved into the nursing quarters at the hospital. The day I moved in I met Kane who lived two doors up from my room. We hit it off instantly and have been together ever since. I was there to study and Kane was there as a part of the new graduate program offered to nurses who had just finished their degrees. Kane had a strong interest in surgery and was working in the surgical unit.

After I finished the midwifery program Kane and I moved back to the city to gain experience in a tertiary teaching hospital. The smaller hospital was wonderful for training but I realised I needed to get exposure and experience with women going through more complicated pregnancies and for this I needed to work in a tertiary referral hospital.

The city hospital was a large teaching hospital and I worked with a variety of women experiencing unusual complications. Women with babies requiring surgery after birth were cared for there and I had the opportunity to experience situations which some midwives only read about. Not that it made me happy, in fact it was the opposite, some of the situations were devastating, but I saw the hope women were given with the new medical advances that teaching hospitals put into practice. I also worked with couples with fertility issues. After I gained a broad range of experience I turned to the pharmaceutical industry for business experience. I got a job working for a multinational pharmaceutical company, which specialised in women's health. Moving back to the city was giving me everything that I wanted in my career. Kane was thriving in surgical nursing and he had completed a Masters degree in trauma.

I was fast approaching thirty when Kane and I decided to start trying for a baby; I'd done my studying and had a successful career. We had always planned to save travelling until we had kids, so it seemed like the perfect time. I didn't really feel my age until we started to try for a baby and re-read all the statistics about infertility I had covered during my training. I was aware that fertility starts to decline from the age of thirty and takes a steep dive at thirty-five. Oh well, I thought, I've worked in the area, know exactly when to try and I'll easily fall pregnant the first month. Well that failed miserably; so did the second month. After the second failure, I brought a puppy home to Kane's great surprise and became the mother of two dogs. Kane said that this had better not happen every month! Oscar and Mabel became our babies; I even had leave from work to make sure they adjusted to our home.

The following few months saw no more luck on the pregnancy front and we decided that we needed a change of scenery and moved from Sydney to Newcastle. We had always loved Newcastle and as we first met each other on the central coast, it was no surprise to anyone when we decided to move there. Work was transferable and opportunities arose so we took them, sold our house, found another, and in a matter of weeks we had packed, moved and changed jobs. We then discovered I was pregnant. Woo hoo! All had gone to plan.

* * *

My pregnancy was uneventful and I enjoyed every moment of it except the really hot days. Delivering Amelia was another story. After twenty-two and half hours of labour she was pulled out by my obstetrician under instruction from me, yelling that I could not do it anymore. I wish the obstetrician had done that two hours earlier but that's the problem in obstetrics, you are not the obstetrician's only patient and my obstetrician was carrying out an emergency caesarean section and after she finished my delivery another patient was waiting for her on the operating table. Amelia was born at 1.10am and I later found out the obstetrician didn't get to bed until 4am and was standing in front of me at 8am. An obstetrician's life isn't one I would wish for.

I had all the hallmarks of a first time mum, the fears and anxiety of doing the 'right' thing. I had planned to go back to work after four months' maternity leave for two days a week in the women's health team at the pharmaceutical company. I loved my job; it enabled me to travel, meet a lot of people, and it exposed me to the world of business. But I soon found out that juggling motherhood and a career wasn't easy and I took more leave to cope with having a new baby. My prenatal expectations were slightly unrealistic and I fell into the trap that everything was going to be the same except we had a baby. After several months' leave I returned to full time work in my local area. Trying to be a great mum and a great employee took its toll and my marriage suffered. Kane and I went through a terrible time and at one point nearly separated. We gave counselling a go, which thankfully was successful and we stayed together. We then decided to start trying for another baby. We thought it would take about six to twelve months given that it took six the first time and I was two years older. To our surprise I fell pregnant on the first attempt and we were thrilled. I never dreamt that the baby would miscarry. All went well over Christmas and I headed back to my obstetrician the first week in January for a scan. We have twins in the family so I wanted to see if there were one or two babies. I told Kane to stay at home as there was nothing wrong and I wouldn't be long.

When I went in I was expecting to see my obstetrician as I had done last time, but it seems her practice had grown considerably and she now had sonographers doing scans and she was on holidays. That was okay, I just wanted to see the heartbeat and get a picture to take home. I went in and sat down. As the sonographer ran the scanner over my abdomen I couldn't see a heartbeat. I was over seven weeks pregnant and knew that the heartbeat should be visible, and I was also sure of my dates. In a mild state of anxiety I asked where the baby was; no reply. Once again I asked where the baby was and again no reply but a small shake of the head and a lot of staring at the machine. I started to shake and when I asked again she stopped and informed me, 'There is no baby'. With that she said to make an appointment to see the obstetrician in one week and left the room. I made my appointment in a daze and headed home.

I don't remember driving home, but as I walked through the door in tears I told Kane that there was no baby. He asked what was happening and I didn't know myself. It was Friday and I barely made it through the weekend. On Monday I called the obstetrician's office, but again was informed that we had to wait a full week. It was an anxious time but we managed to hold out, because we had no other choice. Kane and I went in for the scan; this time there was a small size baby with a heartbeat of 52 beats per minute – a healthy baby has a heart rate of 100 or more beats per minute at this early stage in pregnancy. We were relieved to see an image of a baby, but the low heart rate was not good news. I was booked in for another scan the following week to check on the baby's development.

Throughout the week I spent hours searching the internet to see what the outcomes were when a baby had a heartbeat of 52 and what I found didn't reassure me. One of my beloved dogs wouldn't leave me alone and followed me everywhere; when I returned for my scan the following Monday it became clear why. The baby had died. I chose to wait for the baby to miscarry, but nothing happened and so I went in for surgery and had a curette. Basically, my obstetrician surgically removed the baby by opening my cervix. I never thought this would happen to me; I wasn't prepared for it at all.

This was the push I needed to make a career change. I didn't like leaving Amelia at day care full time so I called the manager of maternity at the local private hospital and went for an interview and was offered a part time position. I immediately resigned from the pharmaceutical company and started working as a midwife again.

I loved it; I had really missed working with mothers and babies and was so glad to have made the change. I had a new understanding of childbirth since having Amelia and I felt like I could relate even more with women. I also had more confidence and life experience and was looking forward to working in a birthing suite again.

Several months after my miscarriage we decided to try for another baby. It only took one month and I was pregnant. I couldn't believe how lucky we were to get pregnant so quickly. I was scheduled to have a scan at six weeks, but while waiting for this I had some spotting. I was now working with my obstetrician in a professional capacity so I told her what had happened and I had another early scan. The results showed that the baby wasn't the size you would expect and I was booked in for another scan the following week. Once again, my dog wouldn't stop following me around and I guessed that the baby had died. The scan confirmed it but instead of waiting to see if I would miscarry I had a curette the same week.

I couldn't believe this had happened again. I had remained as positive as I could after my first miscarriage, thinking that I had had my one and it wouldn't happen again. I was concerned about how I would react after the anaesthetic because you can sometimes say funny things when you wake up; well I let out how upset I was, so much so that my obstetrician said she would run some tests to find out why the miscarriage had happened.

The tests revealed I had anticardiopilin antibodies, which meant that my body was developing tiny clots that stopped the flow of blood to the placenta and caused me to miscarry. I was puzzled as to why this happened given I had Amelia without complication, but anticardiopilin antibodies can develop without warning. Any future pregnancies would require me to have a daily course of injections to prevent me from miscarrying again.

part one

ben

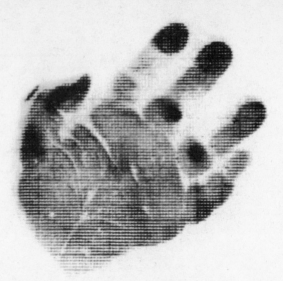

Ben's handprints
and footprints
Date of birth: 03.10.2007

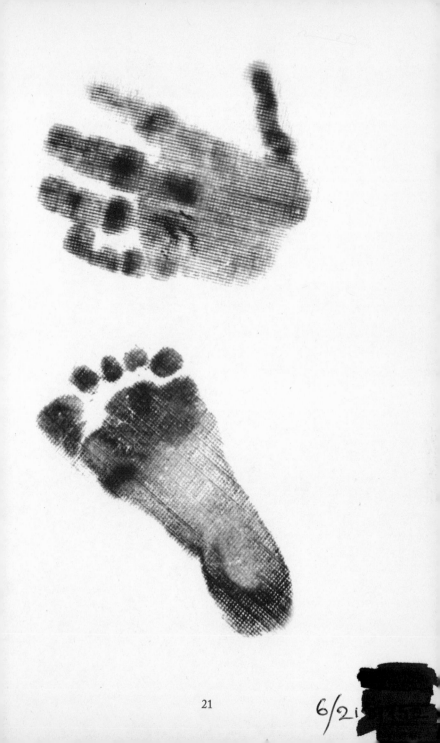

21

6/21

1

I always wanted a baby in the year 2007. Seven is my favourite number. As they say, be careful what you wish for, it might just come true.

It was the beginning of the October long weekend. I was mentally exhausted from my recent promotion to antenatal class coordinator and being a busy mum to Amelia. It was only Saturday morning. I got up early to organise Amelia's breakfast then prepare for the day ahead, teaching ten unsuspecting couples about the agony and ecstasy of birth. I loved teaching these classes; I like to think I made them light-hearted and fun. Women expecting their first baby are often caught up in worrying about the process of birth rather than learning what they are going to do when they get the little person home! My non-midwife friends remind me of this when I tell them about antenatal classes. 'Don't forget to focus more on what to do with the baby,' they say. I remind them about their first pregnancy and if they were as concerned about nappy changing, settling and bathing a baby compared to birth at the time. On reflection, they all realise that they were the same. No one seems to be able to think beyond the birth.

That particular day I was more on edge than I had been in a while. It may have had something to do with my precious pregnancy that we had worked so hard for. I was in my twenty-third week after having two miscarriages and we had tried for twelve months to conceive. I was taking Clexane to prevent miscarriage and had been taking a drug called Metformin to assist me to conceive. At sixteen weeks my obstetrician reassured me it was okay to go off the Clexane and on to aspirin as my, 'Difficult time in the pregnancy was over.' The thought went through my mind that the difficult time had not yet begun.

When a woman in my class that afternoon asked me about stillbirth for some reason I responded with more emotion than usual. 'No one can prepare you for this,' I said. 'It is the most devastating event that can happen in your life and for that reason I don't go into depth about it, but we will talk about assisted deliveries such as emergency caesarean sections which prevent this from happening.' Little did I know that in four days time Kane and I would be living this nightmare and realising that what I had been saying was all too true. Nothing can prepare you for losing a child.

After teaching the class, I returned home to finish preparations for Kane's birthday party. It was a great night, all of us celebrating with Sing Star. A friend later commented how glowing and happy I looked, and how she was so happy for us as a family to be having a baby boy. I went to bed early as I needed to be prepared for work the next morning – you never know what you are going to have to face in a birthing suite; some days are frantic and some very quiet. Thankfully, my shift was quiet, only a couple of pregnant women came in for assessment and reassurance that their babies were okay. But when it is quiet you know that it's the calm before the storm and there was a hurricane on the way. At the end of the shift I headed home, feeling tired and drained.

When I got home I plonked myself on the lounge. I felt ill, nauseous and had some lower back pain. I rested for a couple of hours, the same advice I would give any pregnant woman, dozing on and off and thinking I was just reeling from the hectic social and work activities of the past couple of days. Towards dinner time I felt a bit better. I went to the loo and discovered three small spots of blood. It was bright blood but nothing else followed and I counted Ben's movements inside me; all appeared okay. I called the midwife who I had just left at work for my own reassurance. When I described the physical symptoms logically, there was nothing wrong; no more bleeding, nausea or pain and Ben was moving around. I thought that there was no reason to go in to hospital – my usual obstetrician was away and there's nothing quite like having the on-call obstetrician, who you have never been to as a patient, examining you and then rocking up the next day to do a birth together, knowing that they have seen you in all your glory! Like hell I was going in if I didn't absolutely have to!

The next morning I woke up knowing there was something gravely wrong; a spot in the depth of my stomach ached with the inner knowledge that Ben was dying. When Kane asked me why I was so 'off' that day, I told him Ben was dying. He couldn't believe that I had said that. I called the hospital and the same midwife I had spoken to about my concerns the day before invited me in for reassurance.

On examination, Ben's heartbeat was normal, which I knew it would be because I could still feel him moving but my heart told me it wouldn't be long before he passed away. On my way out from the birthing suite I took some swabs that we use as an initial indicator for women who we suspect may have ruptured their membranes. I thought I would test the loss I was having; it wasn't fluid as such but a slight discharge. All three swabs were positive indicating that the waters around my baby had leaked. That meant that Ben was at risk of an infection which could bring on labour. I again went to the birthing suite where a more definitive test was carried out. The results this time were inconclusive. On my way out I said to the midwife, 'I'm not feeling pregnant now.'

These feelings continued the next day. I called my obstetrician's office to organise a scan on the day she returned from holidays. I was offered a consultation with the on-call obstetrician but knew that all the tests had been done and they could do nothing else. As I hung up the phone the thought went through my mind that I wasn't going to make it until my obstetrician returned to work. The rest of the day was eerie. Amelia went to dancing and swimming lessons and we met up with friends. I sat with my friend who was feeding her baby and talked about how I couldn't see myself feeding my baby; I knew that it wasn't going to happen. Amelia and I went home. I decided to rest because I was still feeling ill. This was the last official day Ben was alive inside me; it was also Kane's birthday.

2

Waking up on Wednesday 3rd October 2007 was like any other day, except I had to wear a pad, as the discharge I was having was thick and I did not want it showing through my clothes. I dropped Amelia off at day care, got petrol for the car and headed to work – but it turned out to be only for a half day as I felt so sick. I had a busy day planned coordinating the antenatal classes and as I walked through the birthing suite I noticed it was packed with women; of all the days I needed this one to be quiet. The midwives ran between rooms and I lent a hand with assessments in between doing my work for the antenatal classes. I spoke with the maternity educator who later said I looked like a frightened child that morning. I went to the loo and was petrified when I saw green fluid on my pad. It wasn't long before I started having pains.

Actually, I had been cramping on and off all morning. I spoke with another midwife in between her caring for other women who bluntly told me to see the obstetrician on duty before I regretted it. I needed that push. I was so frightened, I didn't know what to do, who to tell or where to go. I called the obstetrician who saw me immediately. A mother and her new baby were sitting in his waiting room and she commented that I looked like I wanted to be anywhere else but there. She will never know how right she was. I couldn't even sit on the chair properly because I was so frightened. I had a scan and was reassured that all was okay, but had more tests done in the birthing suite to be sure. I knew what they were and what they would show. I had to wait for a room as it was so busy. I'm sure the other midwives had no idea what was happening to me, judging by the look on their faces when they saw me half an hour later. I couldn't sit down; I was contracting every three minutes and felt like I needed something to help me with the pain. I hadn't called Kane who had taken a day off work and was at home. I didn't know what to say or do, other than go with what my body was telling me – have this baby.

The midwife finally got me on the bed. I hated pulling my pants down in front of my work colleagues but I knew there was no choice. The obstetrician examined me and tried to get the midwife's attention, who had turned away to respect my privacy, but the emergency at hand took over. I was in labour.

I screamed with shock and disbelief so loudly the midwives heard me in the next room. Now it was clear to everyone what was happening. Not again, not another baby, not Ben, was all I could think of as I howled into my hands. Then a thousand thoughts ran through my mind. I thought of the class I had taught last weekend; the first woman I had looked after who lost her baby; how young I was then and how I had no idea of what she had gone through until now. I suddenly realised I hadn't called Kane and asked for the phone. I interrupted him hanging the washing out – I remember finding it the next day, still wet in a basket on the floor. While Kane made his way to the hospital, I arranged for Amelia to be picked up by a friend and called our parents.

In the meantime the midwives went into overdrive. My situation was getting worse and I could feel the warmth of the green fluid running down my legs, like a tap. My waters had broken, and the midwives tried to stop the labour and transfer me to the tertiary hospital, which had the facilities to resuscitate babies born prematurely. Kane arrived to a disaster zone and he held onto me the whole time, reassuring and protecting me the best way he could. He held me through the pain of each contraction and let me squeeze him as hard as I liked without complaint. It wasn't long before I was in an ambulance and at the birthing suite of the tertiary hospital. I recognised the bereavement room; I knew this from a tour I had done when considering which hospital to work in.

The drugs to stop the labour no longer took effect and the pain was intense and ongoing. In desperation I called my usual obstetrician's rooms to ask if they could send the scans she had done to the on-call doctors as I knew Ben was big for his age. Not long after I screamed, 'The baby is coming!' The obstetrician examined me and informed me that I was only two centimetres dilated, had no presenting part of the baby in my pelvis and advised I could be like this for days. I pleaded for an epidural, then pleaded for a caesarean; the answer was no. I couldn't express my exasperation through the pain; I just wished for someone to put me out of my misery. I remember thinking, 'Don't move that delivery trolley, this baby is coming.' All through this Kane was holding me and trying to speak with the nurses and doctors who were on standby to resuscitate Ben. Trying to take in everything the doctors were saying about premature babies was impossible. All I knew was that Ben was dying. Kane and I decided if Ben showed signs of life the doctors should try to resuscitate him. The resuscitation table was set up and the neonatologist and nurse consultant called. I went from only two centimetres dilated to feeling like something was coming within the hour. Ben was in the breech position and his feet were presenting first. This was not unusual for a premature baby. As the obstetrician examined me again I nearly went through the wall with pain as he stretched my cervix. He had a very concerned look on his face as I finally had a break in contractions. He leant over and said, 'You really need to push with the next contraction.' I knew what he meant. I had seen the instruments used to assist births in the birthing suite in a hospital I had worked in previously and I did not want them used on Ben's head. I knew I had to push him out of my cervix which wasn't fully dilated. Christ, I wanted someone to get me out of there. I waited and waited for that final contraction – it was the longest break in pain I had had through my labour – Ben's way of saying leave me be, let me sleep. As the next contraction approached I braced myself for pushing and with one push he was born, and silence filled the room. The quiet voice of the neonatologist informed us that his heartbeat was feeble and only registered 60 beats per minute. Ben slept and we assumed that he died shortly after birth. It wasn't until three days later that we discovered he lived for 57 minutes. If only I had known I would have held him until he drew his last breath. Instead he died alone on a resuscitation table. It will haunt me for all the days of my life.

3

I felt so much better for having delivered Ben. My physical being followed my own intuition and I was pain free. I was also in a state of shock combined with pride and love for my baby. I was proud to give him to my parents to hold, he was beautiful. I loved to see him and hold him as much as any other mother. The only difference was that we were visited by a minister and geneticist. The geneticist was very respectful and advised us that there was no need for autopsy as he couldn't see anything genetically wrong. I was glad for this as it meant I could hold him for as long as I wanted, he didn't need to be refrigerated for extensive periods. It's unnatural the things you are grateful for. We said a blessing with the minister and the family left. Kane wasn't keen to see him as he preferred to remember him as he was born; all I wanted to do was spend as much time with him as possible. Before Kane left the hospital we had time to talk and one of the things we said was that we would try again to have a baby in six months' time.

The midwife bathed and dressed Ben and I cuddled and kissed him as much as I could. There was one thing that kept going through my head about his physical appearance and that was his black foot, which was the result of bruising during the birth. I couldn't help but think if he had lived he would have ended up having one leg; strange things go through your mind. During the night I drifted in and out of sleep with Ben on my chest. As the morning approached I realised that I had to let go of him and I felt a surge of panic wash over me. I wanted to hold my baby forever, to take him home just like I had done with Amelia. I didn't want to be a part of this club that I had not chosen to join. But I had to face the world.

Walking out of the birthing suite was the first time I felt grief with the full force of reality. Kane held me as I felt myself almost collapse. I couldn't understand why everyone was moving so fast. Time was so still in my world. We made it to the car and had to go and pick Amelia up. We wondered what on earth we were going to tell her; we had no idea. We were still fighting the reality that Ben wasn't with us anymore and couldn't imagine explaining this to a three year old when we couldn't understand it ourselves.

We pulled up at our friends' home and their daughter was the first to notice I wasn't pregnant anymore. Quickly we got Amelia and drove home. All we could do was say that baby Ben had gone to heaven and was up in the stars and not in Mummy's tummy anymore. At least she could see this and know that physically he wasn't with us anymore. I was so bloody angry that we had to explain death to a toddler and that she had to watch us go through the agony and pain of grief.

4

In the days leading up to Ben's funeral we received many bunches of flowers, cards and gifts from family and friends. They were beautiful and I have kept the cards to remind me of how thoughtful and caring they were. Our home looked and smelt like a florist. It was during this time that my obstetrician returned from her holidays and called me after she had heard what happened. We spoke for about an hour of the events and it was during this conversation that I remembered a dream I had had nineteen weeks into my pregnancy. I was lying on the bed in room three in the birthing suite at the hospital where I worked, lying on my side crying, the on-call obstetrician and two midwives were standing around me and I didn't know where Ben was. This is exactly what had happened; even the same midwives were there. Ben had been telling me since early in the pregnancy that he wasn't going to live and had been preparing me for the inevitable. My first instinct that something was wrong had occurred at nine weeks when I walked past a board full of photographs of babies in the doctors' rooms; it went through my mind that my baby was not going to be there.

Planning Ben's funeral was done with mixed emotions. Kane and I had complete control over how we would farewell our little boy, which was partly a good thing, but it also meant we had to decide what to cremate him in, what would go with him in the intense heat that would melt his flesh to nothing, leaving only crushed bone. I couldn't bear the thought of my little boy burning; I couldn't bear the thought of him dissolving into the earth. I felt dizzy and desperately wanted to stop this insanity, but also wanted to give Ben the farewell he so deserved. It was overwhelming; all I wanted to do was scream, 'What have I done to deserve this?'

The night before the funeral Kane's family came to stay. It was good to see them even under these circumstances. I love them very much but I didn't anticipate and wasn't prepared for the usual family disorganisation. I didn't know they were bringing their new puppy, a border collie and about an hour into their stay I snapped as I couldn't stand the chaos being caused by their dog and our two chasing around. It was the only time in the entire week that I really wanted some peace. I felt tense, my heart ached and I wanted the world to swallow me whole.

The following morning went so quickly, I felt numb and couldn't believe what was happening. Never in my wildest dreams did I think this would happen. When we got to the chapel, I felt nothing except extreme distress and sadness. If I hadn't been numb from shock, I don't think I could have gone through with it. I can't recall the majority of conversations I had with family and friends that day. Nineteen people attended Ben's funeral, only those who were there on the day we lost him. Originally we had just planned to invite our immediate family, but changed our minds after our close friends asked about the arrangements. They were grieving too. There were many hugs, kisses and tears. The one thing that sticks in my memory is of the beautiful scenery around the chapel and gardens. There were rolling hills, ducks swimming on ponds and birds singing. The weather was perfect. The chapel had glass walls and was a lovely environment for the farewell of our little boy, a place where he would love to have played and where Amelia was enjoying the surrounds oblivious to the sorrow we all felt.

As we approached the entry to the chapel we saw the funeral car with Ben's tiny coffin on the back seat. I didn't know they even made them that small. Kane lifted him out and trembling, together we walked him down the aisle.

It was a simple and respectful farewell to a life not fulfilled or given a chance. We had a lovely minister who read appropriate scripture and gave everyone some beautiful thoughts for the day. To the less religious and spiritual among us it was a relief to hear him say that even though in Christian faith many people believe things happen for a reason, there was no reason for this tragedy. You could hear the sigh of relief among us. Kane and I lit a candle for Ben which Amelia later blew out – our way of including her in Ben's farewell. Blowing out candles was her favourite thing at the time as it reminded her of birthdays. Kane and I also stumbled through some poetry. As we were reading Amelia came to the front of the chapel and asked us not to be sad. Then everyone broke down. Kane read the poem *Yesterday, Today and Tomorrow* which asks us to focus on one day at a time. And I read *The Butterfly Box*;

> *Don't weep at my grave,*
> *For I am not there,*
> *I've a date with a butterfly*
> *To dance in the air.*

I wanted to believe that Ben was happy and safe in a lovely place where he was free to do the things children do. I hoped he was flying through the clouds, playing with balloons, and free from pain. I hoped that he was playing with the other children in heaven. Not long after the funeral I had a dream about a small group of children huddled in a group playing as I stood at the edge watching them. The circle parted and Ben was in the middle with his eyes wide open and laughing as they tickled him. I tried desperately to reach for him and pull him into my arms but no matter how far my arms stretched I couldn't reach him. I took this dream as a sign that he was doing what I so hoped and that he was very happy.

We all farewelled Ben by placing a single white rose on his tiny coffin to Eric Clapton's *Tears in Heaven*. Amelia blew the candle out and Kane and I stayed to have one last moment with Ben. Eric Clapton gave way to *Golden Slumbers* by The Beatles, performed by Ben Folds Five. I gave Ben a final kiss to the words, 'Golden slumbers fill your eyes, smiles awake you when you rise, sleep pretty darling do not cry and I will sing a lullaby.' I started to walk out of the chapel but had to turn back to have one more minute, one more kiss, one more touch and a final look at Ben. It reminded me of being a child begging my parents for one more go at a favourite activity or game. The one more time could have gone on forever. It was a long walk out of the chapel and as I turned my head for the last time his coffin was being carried away by the big, burly man who was to cremate him.

part two

aftermath

5

We were driven home by family members and I was in a daze about what we had just done. A hundred questions ran through my head. Why couldn't Ben come too? Why was this happening to us? What had we done in this world that was so bad that we were being punished like this? I was numb. I had never experienced such sadness – a sadness you wouldn't wish on your worst enemy.

Once home, surrounded by friends and family, I changed completely. I ran around talking about Ben, making sure everyone had somewhat of a good time, showing his picture and the things we had collected for him as if he was with us. I showed him off as any mother would; the only thing missing was him. I had just lain to rest my dead baby and there I was running around like a fool showing him off. I constantly checked that the flowers from Ben's coffin were in enough water to preserve them for the florist who would be drying them for framing. After everyone had gone home I slipped back into my daze, not knowing what to do and waited for the night to fade into a blur of nothingness.

The following days were spent organising the final matters after the funeral. I delivered the flowers to the florist for drying, then I went to work to organise my maternity leave. I did not expect there to be any problems, I just had to sign a few things and go, although other people had protested that I did not have to do this just yet. I had no idea what they were talking about until I drove in to the hospital and it hit me that I was going back to the place where it all began. What had I been thinking? Seriously, I thought I was losing my mind. I was going through two parallels of reality, one was a daze and the other was demanding that I just got on with it. As I parked the car I wondered how I was going to walk through the door but as I did one of my colleagues was walking by and saw me. I talked to her about how I was feeling. My heart was racing, I was sweating and in a state of sheer panic. She led me to the manager's office and we talked for a while, not just about Ben but also about other things. It was a good distraction for a short time. But I had to face going back into the birthing suite and she offered to walk with me through the door. It was such a simple gesture but it made life that little bit easier. As I walked through the door, I realised that the anticipation was worse than the actual event. I wasn't there for long and didn't have to sign a single form. I was fortunate enough to have employers who just put the wheels in motion and sorted out the maternity leave for me. I spoke to a few more people in my daze and then went home.

Grief affects people in different ways. My grief caused me to have moments of rage and Kane was made all too aware of this after an incident in a shopping centre. We were going down an escalator when we saw a mother push her newborn baby in a pram on to it, clearly ignoring the safety notices. I was so angry I exploded, 'What do you think you are doing?' (Along with a few other expletives!) Kane was shocked and pulled me away from the situation as the other mother didn't like what I was saying. I was also angry towards women who smoked and used drugs in their pregnancy. I didn't think it was fair that they went on to have babies who lived despite filling their bodies with dangerous chemicals. Now I realise that these women had their own sets of problems and reasons for their behaviour but then I just wanted to scream with the injustice of it all.

Not long after Ben's funeral I received a phone call from my obstetrician asking Kane and me to come in for the results of the tests to find out what infection had caused me to go into labour. Without hesitation we made our way into her office and went straight in. She explained to us that I had contracted an infection called chorioamnionitis through the placenta and also said that there were no other results from the pathology companies my swabs had been sent to. Perplexed, she had investigated this further only to discover that there was no record of any specimens admitted to the laboratory for testing. I was furious – in all my years as a midwife I had never seen this happen. How could two pathology companies not test such important specimens? Weren't they marked correctly? Did someone just decide to throw them away? Were the tests even sent? Didn't the staff know what to do with the samples? If they were in my position they would want to know what infection had killed their child. Later people commented that it didn't make any difference to the outcome; Ben was so premature he wouldn't have survived and so on. I don't know why they said such pathetic things; it only made me more angry. One friend knew that this was unacceptable. She was a midwife who had worked overseas and told me that people were sued for much less than that. While I had no intention of litigation, I valued her empathy and validation that what happened was wrong. I felt numb and as if I couldn't take any more emotional blows and I went back to living my life in a daze.

* * *

Somehow Kane and I managed to make a lovely collection of memorabilia for Ben. I had to try and do something positive to combat the anger I was feeling at the world. Kane picked a lovely wooden box to put all Ben's things in. I included his hospital wristbands, hat, booties, photo album, his dummy, clothing, wrap, candles and an angel. I have added to it since his death – Christmas decorations and a few other treasures. Creating the box was something positive I was able to do for my little boy; I love going through these things when I want to remember him. After filling his box, I tied a blue ribbon around it to complete it. As I was doing so I recalled a session I once had with a clairvoyant. I had seen the box before. It was a gift from my grandmother. I specifically remembered it because the clairvoyant had said I would have a girl and I was sure the box – with a blue ribbon around it – represented a boy. I have always believed in the spiritual world, but until then, I had not experienced anything so intense, so real; my gut feelings and dreams became real. Recalling this session reminded me I had bought a pack of angel cards from the clairvoyant. I found it at the back of my chest of drawers and each day I started drawing a card from the pack. Each card gave a meaningful and inspirational saying that momentarily lifted my spirits and gave me strength.

After finishing my course of antibiotics, I still felt unwell. I enlisted the help of some alternative therapies and decided to try acupuncture. It was successful in helping to relieve some of the anxiety and depression I was feeling. One thing my acupuncturist noticed each visit was a warm presence in my uterus.

***

Shortly after Ben had passed away, I decided to go back to see the clairvoyant; I wanted to do anything to have contact with Ben again, to feel his presence, to talk to him. I walked through her door and was shocked when the first question she asked me was, 'Who's Benji?' I broke down in tears. The reading was sombre and all about Ben's passing. It was fascinating to hear her say 'Benji' as that was my nickname for him, Enji Benji, after a children's cartoon character. She told me that he loved having me as his mother and he loved his name. Our souls would be together for an eternity but he wasn't going to come back to me. She said that Ben took six hours to leave the earth and asked how long he had lived. I replied that it was one hour. Puzzled, she asked how long my labour was; it was exactly five hours. He had died free from pain and through the clairvoyant he reminded me that he had told me throughout the pregnancy that he wasn't going to stay. The constant anxiety, dreams and premonitions now made more sense. This was the first turning point in my grief.

I had spoken with my baby and he was safe, had died pain free and loved me as much as I loved him. Along with talking to my baby, she also made some predictions for the future, firstly that I would be pregnant again in six months and secondly that I was going to be told that I needed a hysterectomy. Great, I thought. That's all I need.

While the clairvoyant helped me, I still had to face the fact that Ben was not coming back. I was still in shock and couldn't face the reality while I had a medical problem. The rawness of my grief kept showing through. One of these times was at a friend's wedding; celebrating among a large group of people was the last thing I had in mind only a month after Ben dying. I felt uncomfortable before I had left the house because trying to find something to wear was a nightmare. I put on a brave face and off we went. The wedding was beautiful but the entire time all I could think when people looked at me was if they were thinking that I was the person whose baby had just died. I didn't know who knew and who didn't; clearly more people didn't. When people asked me, in polite conversation, how many children I had, I didn't know what to say. I ended up saying that I had two, but one had just died, proceeded to lose the plot and left the room with Kane following behind trying to console me. I spent the rest of the night in the daze that my life had become. I couldn't even drink alcohol to numb the pain because of the large doses of antibiotics I had started taking again as the infection in my uterus still remained. I just wanted to go home to bed – some guest I turned out to be!

The following day I had to pick Amelia up from my parent's house, who lived about three hours away from me. The drive gave me time to think, which wasn't always a good thing. My grief was all consuming; there wasn't a minute I didn't think about Ben and what he would have been like if he had lived. Would he still be on a respirator? Would the infection have healed? Would he have survived? Would he have been disabled? The thought of his black leg kept playing in my mind and I wondered if he had lived would he have had it amputated? My grief was endless and exhausting.

Going to Mum's house turned out to be another turning point in my grief. It was the first time I got a full night's sleep since Ben's death. There's something reassuring about returning to your family home. I headed straight for the fridge, seeing if my favourite foods were there, knowing where Mum hides all the good chocolates and of course, the familiar Tupperware with the Vita Weets and nuts, always a last resort! There was also the familiar smell of the towels and sheets. I don't know what she does to them but they are always so crisp and fresh. My aunty and uncle were there too and my aunty had just finished her midwifery training so we got to have a good old chat about things. Going to bed that night was easy, as Mum, Amelia and I kicked Dad out to the single mattress usually reserved for Amelia and we all slept together. It was another familiarity from childhood, as Mum and I had slept together for years. The next night it was just Amelia and me in the bed, but I enjoyed another full night of sleep. With a good sixteen hours of sleep under my belt, Amelia and I packed up and headed home.

Our sleeping routine at home had changed dramatically. Kane now slept in Amelia's bed while Amelia and I slept in Kane and my bed. I just wanted to be close to her and she could sleep with the television going. The TV was one purchase we made the week after Ben died; I needed it to sleep. I would go to sleep watching my favourite program, *Law and Order*, wake at 3am, watch the show again and fall asleep. I don't know why I liked it so much, but I bought all six series and it helped me through many nights of torment.

6

I went to the acupuncturist for another treatment and again she identified the heat in my uterus that she couldn't explain. I was also sweating all the time, soaking the sheets overnight, drenching my clothes and constantly wiping my face down. There was something very wrong and I decided to call my obstetrician. She sent me off for some blood tests; she couldn't understand why my uterus would still be infected as I had taken four courses of different antibiotics. The results that came back were puzzling. All my infection markers were normal but the inflammation markers were above normal range. She advised me that I would need to see an immunologist as there was possibly an underlying autoimmune problem. 'You're kidding me,' I thought, as I made an appointment to see my family doctor for a referral.

In the meantime I hit the internet and looked up everything associated with high inflammation markers. I found some serious disorders that frightened me to bits, as well as some less serious diseases, like pelvic inflammatory disease. Well that made sense to me; I had just given birth and had a nasty infection. Armed with this new information off I went to my family doctor. I sat there in a state of angst discussing my internet findings with tears pouring down my face. When my doctor asked me what I would like her to do, I pleaded for a full pelvic examination and if that revealed nothing, then I wanted a referral to a specialist. She agreed.

Sure enough there was fresh, bright spotting and pain on examination, and so she organised a scan with my obstetrician. My obstetrician was also a specialist in foetal medicine and scanned not only her own patients but those of other obstetricians as well. I had my scan two days later and my obstetrician found my uterus full of old blood, retained placenta and a bright flashing spot that looked like Christmas lights. I had no idea what it was, but the look on her face told me she was puzzled. We arranged for a dilation and curettage (D and C) – a surgical procedure to remove part of the lining and the contents of the uterus – to clear the retained products and then off I went.

I was to go to hospital the following morning, so with Amelia at day care I headed to the shops for new PJs. It was only when Kane called and asked what I was doing that it hit me. Having a D and C takes only a short amount of time. I said to him that there was something terribly wrong and that I wouldn't be coming home from hospital. I told him I was going to bleed and they would have to do a hysterectomy. I panicked. I had had these premonitions before when Ben was dying. I dropped everything and went home to call my doctor. By this stage I was sobbing. I felt sorry for the administration staff who had to listen to me rant that I was going to need a hysterectomy and lose my uterus if I had the D and C. When my obstetrician called me back she said, 'You must have some kind of ESP Nicole. When you phoned I was on the phone to a doctor at Westmead Hospital discussing the bright spot on the scan. If I do the D and C tomorrow the events that you are talking about could very well happen.' My obstetrician told me I had a rare condition called a uterine arterio venous malformation. When I explained this to my doctor she said she had read about the condition in a text book, but had never seen one in her practice. I was in shock; she had studied at some of the biggest teaching hospitals in Australia and overseas. My instructions were to come back the following week for another scan to see if it had changed.

I hit the internet again and what I saw didn't impress me. Uterine arterio venous malformation was a rare disorder with only one hundred documented cases in literature.

There was nothing of substance that I could rely on to say if I would have another baby. In some cases a hysterectomy was necessary. The literature concluded that the disorder was linked to having D and Cs and infection. Well I had had both. I had a D and C after each miscarriage and had caught an infection after the last one. However, there was one story of a woman with recurring arterio venous malformations and she did have children; this at least gave me some hope. I also looked at how the condition was treated and found that the most current technique was by a procedure called embolisation, carried out by an interventional radiologist. The procedure involved puncturing the femoral artery and winding a fine catheter through the major arteries down to the problem vessels and destroying the malformed ones. It appeared that this, or surgery with a possible hysterectomy, was my choice.

7

Some of the women in my mothers' group had planned a night out without the kids. I found a lot of support in my group except that they all had little boys. I didn't really feel like going, but made myself go in an effort to keep on living. It was becoming too easy to just hang around, in bed, watching *Law and Order* over and over, even though that was exactly what I wanted to be doing. There were lots of conversations going on around me but I really didn't feel a part of any, hearing them talk about their baby boys and the chaos they bring to their homes. I found myself thinking how different my chaos was. I didn't really know what to talk about, so I found myself staring into space most of the time, not wanting to talk because of fear that the other mothers would not want to hear about my dead baby and that the pub wasn't really an appropriate place to do so. It was a voluntary withdrawal from conversation, as I did not want to bring it down and kill the jovial atmosphere. I felt left out and alone.

No matter how a baby dies, there is always a level of self-hatred and self-blame. Even though I couldn't control the underlying problem, it was my body that had failed Ben. I felt that I had let him and my family down. I wanted to escape. I couldn't see how I fitted in with my friends and family anymore. As I turned the corner and into the drive way in front of my house later that evening, I contemplated packing a bag and leaving, I didn't know where, but just driving and seeing where the road took me. If it weren't for my precious Amelia, I may just have done it. Amelia kept me alive, even though that was a responsibility way beyond her purpose in life. If it weren't for her I don't know where I would be. Amelia made me get up each morning, to get breakfast, lunch and dinner.

* * *

My life had turned into a task-orientated drill. I made notes for myself to get up, do the washing, buy milk and sometimes I just wrote 'breathe'; just breathe for one more hour, one more day. Things weren't getting any better; in fact they were getting worse. All I could think about was Ben and what life had become. My grief was all consuming, and I doubted that I was ever going to feel okay again. Every day was the same and there was no one who could help me. I only wanted my baby back. I was in such a state of despair that I wanted everyone to go to hell. I was sick of everything. I was sick of the doctors – there wasn't even a doctor where I lived who could help me with my problem. As far as I was concerned, the doctors could get stuffed as well. I was so, so angry. I was angry that my baby had died. I was angry that my daughter had to learn about death at such a young age. I was angry that the laboratories threw my swabs away so I will never know what killed Ben, and I was most angry that I didn't know he had lived for an hour. I was livid. And the world could go to hell.

* * *

Despite my messed up mental state, I managed to make myself go to the gym. It was a great outlet for my anger. I rode up the hills on the bike and for the first time I managed a jog on the treadmill. With each extra stride and ounce of pain, my anger at the universe for dealing me this hand dissipated. I also cried, a lot, and I didn't care who saw. Being able to let out the emotion stopped my head from exploding and my wanting to pull out my hair, because at times the pain was unbearable.

My anger wasn't just directed at people making thoughtless comments – such as those who asked me how many children I had. On a good day, I'd respond politely, but God help those who asked on a bad day – but also towards the Australian medical system. I went back to my obstetrician's office anxious to hear her thoughts on how to fix my problem. My distress increased and I started to panic at the thought of having a hysterectomy and becoming infertile as a result. I remembered the plans Kane and I had made in the birthing suite after having Ben; we'd agreed to give it six months and try again. I wanted someone to tell me it was going to be okay, not to worry, there won't be any problem, you will have another pregnancy without hiccups, and you will give birth to a beautiful girl, full of life. Instead, people started saying things like, 'Why don't you consider adoption?' or 'You already have one healthy child, that's enough.' It seemed as if I was the only one holding on to hope.

* * *

Going in for the scan to check on the malformed vessels that were in my uterus, I decided I wanted to see an obstetrician whom I had worked with in Sydney. His name came to me the weekend before I had Ben, when out of the blue an old friend from Sydney had dropped by with her new son and she mentioned he had been to her obstetrician. I felt he could help me. He had a vast range of experience and was a very pleasant and kind doctor as well. As my obstetrician scanned me she gave me the good news that all the old placenta and blood had passed, my ovaries appeared normal, I was ovulating again, and the inflammation had settled down. So far, so good I thought. But, as soon as she flicked the monitor to colour, the Christmas tree appeared – there was no change to the arterio venous malformation. I was angry again. She advised me that there were doctors at the public hospital who could operate, but I would have to consent to a laparotomy and/or hysterectomy. I looked at her and said, 'Under no circumstance is anyone to touch my uterus with a knife.' I then asked if she could call the obstetrician in Sydney on my behalf and she agreed. When she said that she would try next week, I was still looking at her and then said she would try tomorrow.

I felt relieved and guilty because she was trying to help me and all I did was act like an idiot. I guess that had something to do with the suggestion of a hysterectomy. That was not an option for me; I was not in a life or death situation. I left my appointment feeling scared and worried about my ability to have another baby. This was a distraction I really didn't want at this stage because it was taking the focus off Ben and Amelia. Once again my resilience was being put to the test and I didn't know how much more I could take.

To add to it all, on the following weekend, Amelia spent Sunday afternoon playing out on the back deck on her scooter. Without hesitation she flew down the three steps head first – and slammed into a paver. In one knock her front tooth came out root and all, blood was everywhere. She was shocked and screamed blue murder. I wondered what else could possibly go wrong. Thankfully, the tooth fairy visited that night and so some of the wrong was righted.

That night I experienced the usual lack of sleep. I got about five or six hours of broken rest, lulling myself back to sleep with the gongs on *Law and Order*. The next day I felt no better, so when I got out of bed I started writing my back-to-basics lists. I had used the technique of list writing in many aspects of my life, especially work-related matters, or when I was trying to lose weight. It was a way of making me prioritise what I needed to do. My lists became a tool for getting me through the day. I wrote lists to remind myself to breathe, get up, do the dishes, get dressed. I also made notes of what was good, bad and ugly to try and put some perspective on things.

In the past Kane and I had used this technique to aid us in making decisions about careers and moving house. I found this worked for a short while – I remembered I was ovulating normally again and that went under the 'good' but the rest fell under the 'bad' and 'ugly' pretty quickly when I remembered that I may not have a uterus to carry another baby. Then my obstetrician called to say she had tried but failed to get hold of the other doctor I wanted to see. I snapped at her and immediately afterwards regretted it – she was doing her best to help me. I forced myself to stay at home as Kane and I had been so busy running around to doctors' appointments and such that we'd fallen behind with the housework. I am not a person who enjoys housework but finishing it on that day made me feel as if I had accomplished something. I spent hours tidying and cleaning, and then went through Ben's box. I hugged and kissed his urn and had a one-sided conversation with him. It helped me to feel his presence.

I felt a little better towards the end of the day – a good thing happened when I went to the gym. I found I was able to use a machine I was normally too big for as my breasts were settling down from lactating. That or the exercise I was doing was paying off. I was really pleased. When I returned home, I selected an angel card from my pack, which told me to ground myself – it was much needed advice given the rollercoaster of uncertainty I was on and the daze I continued to live in. Asleep that night I had a dream that I did have another baby, assurance from my angels that all would be okay.

8

It wasn't long before I got a call from my obstetrician advising me that the doctor I wanted to see in Sydney had agreed to see me as an urgent patient. This meant I would get an appointment quickly, and my problems would be fixed without the need for surgery. Phew!

In the meantime life kept going on. As much as I wanted to disappear, go away, vanish, anything but face reality, time kept moving. My days were spent not just crying but feeling overwhelmingly sad. I made sure Amelia kept her usual routine and it was in doing this that I found great support, especially in her dance group. The parents of the kids in Amelia's dance group had known each other for about a year. We had watched each other's kids grow, had attended each other's birthdays, and talked about all life's ups and downs.

One of the mums even had a baby and we spent every week watching him grow and reach milestones. They were a terrific bunch of people. After Ben died, together with other friends, they took it in turns to make my family meals, handled the hiccups of organising kids' concert dilemmas, ferried the kids to rehearsals – they were a wonderful group of women and I was so thankful and grateful for their support. The staff at Amelia's day care were also tremendous – they even offered to take her overnight if Kane and I needed a break. They had known Amelia for two years and always took her extra early or on different days if need be. But there were also moments that were not so good.

On one occasion I had changed the time of Amelia's swimming lesson so I could attend with a friend and our kids could be together. I really needed someone with me to face the world, but that came at a cost and the need to change swimming teacher. In the group of four, Amelia was the only girl and the newest member. She was not a confident swimmer and absolutely hated having her head under the water. Of course, the bruiser boys had all the confidence in the world and the teacher wasn't impressed that Amelia was not up to their standard. She shook her head, made snide comments and treated her differently by making her go last each time. I was in tears and my friend said to go and wait in the foyer and she would look after Amelia. From the foyer I saw some commotion going on through the large, glass windows, but I couldn't see who was involved. The next moment my friend walked out with Amelia covered in vomit. I was already crying, but now I was sobbing. How could the swimming instructor have forced her to the point of vomiting? I was furious. When the teacher walked out to talk to me, she saw the state I was in, and advised that it really wasn't that bad. Then I told her I had just lost my baby and she reached out and hugged me, covering us all in vomit. Even though she was very empathetic, I decided that Amelia wasn't ready for this kind of treatment and put her back in private lessons.

* * *

Amelia's activities were a distraction but my mind was still on Ben the whole time. Anxiety about the future was eating at me and I drifted around not feeling a part of life, just going through the motions. I couldn't express my feelings verbally so I carried on writing lists under the themes good, bad and ugly. I couldn't talk to my family doctor who in the past had been a help. In fact, for some reason I didn't want to talk to her. I couldn't see logic, reason or cure for this. I didn't want to go to any groups; unless they could bring back Ben, I didn't feel that anyone could help me. The only things that gave me some relief were acupuncture and my reassuring angel cards.

The cards gave me little messages of calm, reassurance and inspiration. So at this point I also started meditation which brought some added relief. It was the first time spirituality had been such a big part of my life. Perhaps it was because I had learned that loved ones watch over us from a different dimension.

9

Seven weeks after Ben died I started having moments when he was not at the front of my mind. This change brought with it a whole new set of emotions, the main one being guilt. It's a strange thing to say, but luckily sadness took over. The shock I experienced protected me from feeling the rawness of grief, so to my surprise, when I thought I would start to feel better, I actually started feeling worse. My grief was like a bleeding wound. I had put a bandaid on and for a moment it stopped bleeding, but the slightest scratch made it start bleeding worse than before.

On the days when my wound was scratched, I found I had to run with the pain and heartache. No bandaids like the gym, eating or shopping could mask my emotions. The pain became worse because I had been delaying the inevitable. I had to face the fact that my baby was not coming back. My family was incomplete and there was nothing I could do. I spent hours lying on my bed, going through the things in his box, smelling his clothing and just cried. I hated it but I couldn't change the way I felt. It was all part of my healing.

10

I had to go to see my obstetrician for a preparatory scan to take to the doctor I had been referred to in Sydney. I was hoping that the malformed vessels would have gone but deep down I knew they were going to be there after my acupuncturist told me the heat was still in my uterus. Sure enough they were there, but on the plus side, all my blood tests were good. It was at this appointment that I realised I wasn't ready to go back to work. While I was waiting to be seen I saw another pregnant lady get her ultrasound pictures of her baby and how elated and happy she and her partner were – they even cheered – while I sat there with tears in my eyes thinking what a load of shit it all is, I don't want to see this. It wasn't me and my baby and I felt angry and envious. I couldn't imagine working in the birthing suite or how I would cope if someone complained about a crying baby in the postnatal ward. Although I missed my work, I realised I was not in the right frame of mind to go back.

The following week I saw my doctor in Sydney. It wasn't quite the reunion I was hoping for but under the circumstances he made me feel well looked after and, most importantly, safe. He knew exactly what to do and who to send me to, better still he called the interventional radiologist at St Vincent's Hospital while I was sitting there. The radiologist agreed to see me in a week and gave me his number just in case I started to haemorrhage. If this was the case, I was to come to Sydney immediately, and he would fix any problem sooner than the scheduled appointment which was still two weeks away. He was very empathetic and knew Kane's and my concerns. The only hiccup was because the condition was so rare, he had only done the procedure five times, and if he felt like he couldn't fix it, I would have to go to Melbourne where they specialised further in this area. Please, I prayed, let me stay in Sydney.

Fortunately the bleeding, although heavy, didn't result in continuous bleeding that would indicate a haemorrhage, and I kept to the scheduled appointment for the procedure. I was vaguely familiar with what was going to take place; people would normally have a similar procedure for cardiac reasons. The surgeon was going to puncture the femoral artery and thread a very long, fine catheter through to the problem vessels in the uterus and blow them up, so to speak. The only problems I had to be concerned about were what they were going to anaesthetise me with, and how on earth was I going to lie still for three hours after the operation

Kane and I travelled down from Sydney and stayed at a motel in the heart of Sydney's notorious Kings Cross. What an eye-opener; I hadn't smelt anything that bad for years! We didn't realise how fortunate we were to live two hours north of Sydney. We made tracks to town and spent a lovely afternoon together walking through Hyde Park and shopping in the Queen Victoria Building. Kane didn't just buy me any flowers but beautiful Pandora flowers for my charm bracelet – flowers that would last forever. We stopped by a bottle shop and picked up a bottle of our favourite champagne, Veuve Clicquot, for when we had our next baby. It was a very special afternoon, but we had to retire early in preparation for the next day and the procedure that was ahead. Kane was as nervous as I was because he had seen complications from these procedures in his career as a nurse. I was oblivious to this as all I was focused on was this being a success so we could have another baby.

We woke early and headed for the hospital. Kane wasn't allowed in to see me so I spent some of the pre-operative time alone. I met with the professor who reminded me of my dad; he was of a similar age and hair colour and spoke with the same authority. I felt at ease immediately. The lovely nursing staff made me feel comfortable and the radiologist was a hoot! He made me laugh which was a welcome relief from the seriousness of the situation. I asked what they were going to give me as an anaesthetic and they responded with, 'A local.' What! I wanted more drugs than that – I wanted to be put to sleep! That was clearly not going to happen, so I looked at the up side; I could see the look on the faces of the staff to see how the procedure was going.

In the needle went. Although I didn't feel the puncture of the major artery I felt the blood pulsating down my leg. It was a most disturbing sensation, but it didn't last long and the procedure commenced. It seemed like ages but it only took about an hour and a half. I had never seen catheters so long. The team amazed me with their professionalism, team work and humour. They operated on me while talking about the rare liver treatments they are currently involved with concerning cancer patients. I was blown away and felt like the routine patient for the day and not the sixth patient the professor had ever carried out the procedure on. At the end I was told that this condition was why I had lost Ben. The radiologist showed me on the nine TV screens the before and after photos of the problem vessels. The first picture looked like a curly pig's tail, and the second was a grey fuzzy screen. I was confident that the malformed vessels had been successfully removed.

Instead of going to the recovery ward I sat in a waiting bay for three hours watching patients come and go, and going crazy from not moving. The staff kept a very close eye on me to make sure I stayed put. One of the nurses said she couldn't believe I stayed so alert throughout the procedure. I replied that I had been constantly looking at her face to see how it was going! We laughed and she offered me pain killers, but I wasn't in pain so declined. I wasn't expecting pain given I had not had any during the operation, but the first time I got up it hit me hard. I could hardly walk. I stumbled out to where Kane was anxiously waiting. As we drove through Sydney's peak hour traffic we were relieved that it was over, and excited to be going to pick up Amelia who had been staying with my mum. The drive home was long and exhausting, and once there I headed straight to bed and slept for most of the night.

The following morning I took Amelia to dance class. This was important as it was the final practice before the end of year concert. It turned out to be a big mistake as I was in so much pain I had to leave the rehearsal early and Kane had to come home from work to pick us up. I took some pain killers and went to sleep. When I woke I realised I had an appointment with my family doctor, so in I went only to be told I should have stayed at home or at least had someone drive me in. I was starting to agree with my doctor as I was quite dizzy and still very tired. I took her advice and went home to bed.

11

With Christmas fast approaching we somewhat awkwardly started socialising again. Our closest friends noticed a change in me that I was unaware of; I was completely ignoring their son. Kane mentioned it to me one night after they left and I had no idea that I had been doing so. I was so upset and I rang them to tell them that it was not intentional and I was very apologetic. Their son was about the same age as Ben would have been and just as our daughters were good friends, we had had great plans for our boys to be great friends too. Obviously I was mourning what would never be, and subconsciously had distanced myself from him. It was the first sign that others were moving on in their grief but mine was still very raw and I needed to talk to others who had experienced this too. It was the first time I wanted and needed help, and so I turned to the organisation, Sudden Infant Death Association or SIDS and Kids. SIDS helps families who have lost a child for many different reasons. The drop-in approach was wonderful and it was a place that I could go and be myself, show raw emotions and not feel like the odd one out.

Around this time, I came across a page in my diary with a phone number and address of a woman I had taken care of who had lost her baby nine months earlier. I had asked if I could call her down the track to check how she was doing. I had not done this before, but I related to her. She had a lovely and supportive family, a son the same age as Amelia and I had just found out I was pregnant with Ben. I ummed and arred about calling but in the end I bit the bullet and phoned. I was so glad I did as it turned out we had had our babies' funerals in the same place, had chosen the same urns, had both dried the coffin flowers and we had a mutual understanding of the pain of losing a baby. We became very good friends and helped each other when it was tough. Sometimes we would sit in silence and not saying anything but knowing what the other was feeling. We went to SIDS and Kids together where we talked, laughed and cried. I mourned losing a son, she mourned losing a daughter yet we still could talk about the woes of parenting our four year olds. We shared our biggest fears about our kids, when we would try to get pregnant again, what if something were to go wrong, what we would do if we had the same sex baby again, and what we could feel if we didn't, feeling safe in the knowledge that we would not judge each other. We formed a friendship that will last for all my days.

That afternoon I started to experience pain in my uterus, pain so bad I took the maximum pain killers I could get from the chemist and was still doubled over. I went to my family doctor and got some stronger pain killers and was reassured by her calling the professor who did the embolisation to ask whether this was expected. It was expected and the pain was the uterus healing where the vessels had been destroyed.

* * *

At home I often found myself daydreaming and just watching Amelia. One day when she was sleeping she looked so angelic the thought crossed my mind about why Ben didn't want to be a part of this. He would have been able to share in a good home with two loving parents and a sister who was kind, generous and very funny. He didn't get a chance to be a part of this and to experience his family in life instead of in death; his only way of knowing us was in a spiritual sense. I felt so alone and as if I was losing the plot. I headed to my local bookshop to find something on grief and stillbirth. There wasn't much choice but there was one book. I bought it, took it home and read it from cover to cover. I cried the whole time and realised that I was completely normal.

Kane and I decided to go away with our friends for a long weekend. I was so eager to get out of the house, to get away from reality for a while. We got some much needed rest away from home; a change of scenery was exactly what we needed. There were still some days I contemplated driving and not stopping. I wondered where I would end up. Would I only make it to another town or state? Then reality would set in and I would drive to day care to collect Amelia and then back home where I got on with my usual routine.

Amelia wasn't always a routine child, and one particular day was no exception. She was turning out to be quite accident prone. After all the dance rehearsals, dance photos and costumes, the morning of the Christmas concert arrived and she fell on her hip during her swimming lesson and bruised it so badly she couldn't perform in the concert. This was just another event in the worst year possible.

The lead up to Christmas was causing me great anxiety – anxiety associated with what was supposed to be a joyful and happy day when all I felt was loss and sadness.

It was time to start preparing for Christmas. I didn't want it to come; I didn't want to have to pretend to be happy; in fact, I hated knowing it was just around the corner. I didn't want presents and cheer. I didn't want trees and lights; I wanted the day to fade but knew I couldn't avoid it, especially with Amelia. It was the first Christmas she understood the concept of Santa and couldn't wait for him to come, so I did the opposite to what I was feeling and went completely overboard and had the house covered in decorations and lights and inflatable Santas on the front porch. I bought Amelia so many Christmas presents that she ended up not being able to open them as it was all too much.

I didn't know how I was going to get through the day. My parents had organised Christmas lunch at a hotel so we would not have to worry about the mess. It was also an opportunity for Amelia to give her dummy to Santa. There was a special Christmas church service for those who had lost loved ones during the year which we attended and we lit a candle in memory of Ben. It was very special as Kane was not a strong believer in religion but attended this service. I found solace in faith and enjoyed attending services. Kane's attendance was an example of how we respected and supported each other in our marriage. One Sunday earlier in the year when I went to church I was taken by surprise to find a baby's christening taking place and I just broke down. The support there was amazing and the church members comforted me before I left. It was these things that reminded me of the good in people and the support that is out there.

Despite my anxiety, Christmas Day turned out to be quite peaceful and relaxing. The build up to the big day was actually worse than the day itself. My parents gave me a beautiful Tiffany's locket necklace with a picture of Ben in it. Amelia gave her dummy to Santa in return for a tiny teddy bear that she would sleep with at night for the next week. We stuck to our guns with this one and didn't cave when she wanted her dummy. It was the only real discipline we stuck to since having Ben. She was getting away with everything and had everything she wanted because we couldn't bear to see her upset. New Year came and went with no celebration, we slept through it, but on January 1, Kane and I felt a shift in time – it was a new day and a new year, what a relief.

12

With the New Year in, I had to return to work. We needed
the money as the baby bonus money had paid for the funeral
and other expenses and had now run out. It was not going to
be easy. One of the hardest questions I knew I would have to
answer was how many children I had. This always came up in
the birthing suite. Some of my colleagues suggested I worked
on the postnatal side, but if one woman had complained that
her child was crying I didn't know what I would do and I
didn't want to work in the special care nursery. I wasn't ready
to face looking after all the premature babies. So I had to suck
it up and work out a way I was going to handle everything. I
planned to evade the issue of the number of children I had in
response to questions, and only talk about Amelia. That way I
didn't have to disregard my son. Women about to have a baby

did not want to hear about Ben.

Exactly three months after having Ben I was rostered to work. It was a morning shift on a weekday so there would be extra staff around if I fell apart. The night before I was rostered I got a phone call warning me that there was a woman having a stillbirth, and I was offered the day off. I decided to go. There was no easy way to return, and I had to get back on the horse. I was a master at avoiding things I didn't like, and was determined not to let this be a barrier. There was always going to be the first time when this happened. My first shift back wasn't ideal, but that's life. There were three stillbirths my first week back.

I walked through the birthing suite door and saw the butterfly immediately. An image of a butterfly on the door of a birthing suite signified that the woman had had a stillbirth. Even though I knew it would be there, it still took my breath away. This particular day I was allocated to a couple having their third baby and the mother was in spontaneous labour. I was relieved – it was a good labour! It was actually wonderful and very healing to see someone have a 'normal' experience; instead of sadness and pain there was joy and happiness. Their family unit was now complete with the loveliest baby; they even sent me a thankyou card for my help and assistance with the birth.

I knew then that I would be okay, that my own grief was

not being expressed in my work. It actually gave me hope about having my third baby too. Unfortunately as wonderful as this was, it was also bittersweet. The obstetrician who also attended this lady's birth was the same person who delivered Ben. He was pleasant and helpful as usual with his patients but he didn't even acknowledge my presence, didn't say hello and after he had delivered the baby, he complained about the trials and tribulations of having children of his own. At that point I was checking the placenta and membranes that surround the baby while in the womb, making sure that they were complete and none had been retained in the uterus after birth. It wasn't the best time to complain about those things and I had to put the placenta back in the bowl and go to the pan room to finish checking it, as I felt like throwing it at him. I was so angry and upset that someone who had seen me at my absolute worst couldn't even say hello and instead complained about their kids. My blood was at boiling point. Thank goodness the staff for the next shift were about to come on and I could go home. At handover, my obstetrician tried to say hello and welcome me back but I was still in shock, and angry about that morning, so I didn't particularly feel like being pleasant, but she snapped me out of the daze I was in and got my attention.

What surprised me the most about going back to work was what people didn't say. I soon realised that people's reactions to grief were unique – everyone grieved in their own way. I had to continue with my grief despite others' discomforts around me. I was surprised that people who regularly came into contact with other people in situations similar to my own were so speechless around me. That is not to say that this was true of everyone. Many had put a collection together and bought me a lovely charm for my bracelet, and I received cards, flowers and many well wishes and hugs. I found that women were most at ease talking about Ben and they gave me tremendous support, comfort and protection particularly when there were women in the birthing suite who were having stillbirths.

Somehow I survived my first few shifts back at work. Most of the time I was in a daze and did not remember what I had done the day before. However, when I was looking after the women I was fine, because it gave me a chance to focus on something other than myself. It also kept me in present time rather than thinking about the past or future. I would have rather had their problems and concerns than mine any day, and while I was caring for them I didn't have to think about what I had been through, or the upcoming medical appointments to check if the malformation in my uterus had gone, or my appointment with the geneticist the following week.

It was around this time that someone made a comment that I will always remember. Someone said to me, 'Don't be a victim.' I was speechless, it had only been three months since Ben's death, and although I was still living in a daze I didn't think I was being a 'victim'. I realised that this response was about her expectation of me but I wanted to say, 'Please let my son's ashes cool before boxing me into a role I know I will not fall into.' If anything I wanted to find good somehow though all the mess and thoughtless comments like this made me realise how little some people knew me. It was a sign that people were moving on in their grief, whereas mine was only just starting. The initial shock had worn off and I was waiting to feel better but I was feeling worse than ever before.

The following week I had my follow up medical appointments. The first one was with my obstetrician who did a scan to see if the malformation had gone. It had been an anxious wait to say the least. To my relief all the malformed vessels had been destroyed. The pain I had at Christmas time had been my uterus healing and it had healed well. I couldn't be more thankful to the team at St Vincent's Hospital. I was also given the all clear to start trying for another baby, but Kane and I decided to wait until I had a regular period before trying again.

The next appointment was with the geneticist's team which included a specialist doctor and counsellor. It was like being back at square one. We saw the same doctor who saw us the day I gave birth to Ben and I was very upset by this. What had also made me upset was that I had had a phone call earlier to let me know that the blood tests done at Ben's birth had been disposed of by the Area Health Service. 'Well,' I said, 'they also threw away the swabs that would have told me what infection killed my baby so why not throw these as well.' It was going to be a short appointment. To my surprise, the counsellor came to greet me with a lovely smile and cheerfully said that I had looked after her when she had a baby. I really didn't know what to say through my tears because I couldn't remember her. I felt bad about this but I was a train wreck with no thoughts other than Ben and an Area Health Service that disposed of both swabs and blood tests related to his death. I felt like someone was doing this on purpose and vowed I would not let this happen to anyone I ever looked after in the same situation. Even my obstetrician commented on how unusual it had been. Through the tears and anger I carried on; it was a short appointment because there were no results to discuss, but it was not totally fruitless. Kane and I were both tested for the cystic fibrosis gene and I had repeat blood tests done. I also found myself looking at the counsellor's career and thinking that I could do that if I wanted to. I had been looking at more education and made a note to investigate this further. A week later I recalled the counsellor, but it wasn't in the postnatal area I had attended her birth. I called her to apologise and let her know the same.

13

It was fast approaching Ben's official due date. It was almost four months since we had lost him. It was starting to sink in that he wouldn't be here in five, ten or twenty years' time and it made me even more upset; not just teary but deeply sad, a sadness I had not felt before, one that sat deep in my stomach and made my heart ache. It continued to keep me up at night and woke me early in the morning. Once again only the distraction of my favourite show could put me back to sleep. I knew I was going to need more help to get through this.

In an effort to keep up appearances and continue to see our friends, we had the same group of friends over that had been with us the weekend before Ben died. It amazes me how lives can change in such a short period of time. We had lost Ben, others had had a book published, twins had been welcomed and were growing fast, and our single friend had a lovely new girlfriend. Everyone else was progressing whereas we were stuck.

Kane and I didn't choose the path we were on. We did not want to join this group that we could never leave. Kane also felt the difference of watching other people progress in their lives while ours remained incomplete. When we talked about it later we realised that this was the deepest pain we would go through and together we would make it. We realised that the feeling of our family being incomplete was something we would have to live with all our days, no matter how many children we had; one would always be missing. We knew we had to get through this to enjoy playing with our daughter again, to go on and have another baby, to keep our marriage and keep living life. I was simply existing rather than living. I forced myself to keep Amelia's routine and forced myself to go to work.

One small thing we did that made an enormous difference was employ a house cleaner. Our house cleaner took very good care of us and always went above and beyond the call of duty so that we kept a somewhat tidy and clean home. I spent a lot of time trying not to think of Ben – some days I would not think of him and then felt guilty. I wondered how I would be able to move on and enjoy life without him.

The only people I could fully explain this to were those who had been in the same situation. Others tried but couldn't understand and when they tried to make sense of it, I only got angry and frustrated. This was the case when I turned to one health professional, who tried to get me to see things rationally. This included the rare medical condition I had and I was not to presume that all medical problems in the future would be like this. I was fuming inside, how dare someone try to rationalise my situation. What if I have another medical scare? Would I not get any tests again? I put on my argumentative hat and before long our session came to an abrupt end. I walked to my car feeling worse than when I had gone in. I fell in a heap and was so distraught that Kane had to come home from work early. SIDS and Kids was around the corner so I drove there first where they gave me the support and comfort I desperately needed. I also went through their library of books and borrowed some that had explanations for my feelings. Through reading I was able to acknowledge that the third and fourth months were the hardest in the grieving process. I was so relieved because I felt worse than ever before. I ended up staying for a while and made an appointment to see their counsellor.

* * *

The first thing I noticed about the counsellor was that it was a man. I immediately wondered how he was going to help me having never been in the position I faced. I was proved very wrong and he turned out to be the best help I could have got. He was calm, quietly spoken and listened. When I told him how abnormal I felt, how I felt like an alien, that people would look at me and say there is the woman with the dead baby, how much panic and anxiety I felt about Ben's due date fast approaching and how sad I felt he asked, 'Why would you expect anything different?' It was like the weight of the world was lifted; of course I would feel like this, I had just lost my baby. He explained that the thing Kane and I feared most had just happened. It was the comfort I felt in the subsequent sessions that allowed me to talk about this and mourn what I called my normal life, what it should have been like. I mourned not being at home with my newborn baby, his big sister kissing his chubby cheeks, walking him in his brand new red stroller, dressing him in his new blue and green outfit, wrapping him in his green muslins and using the matching dummies. I felt that our family was incomplete and the grief consumed my life like never before.

* * *

It didn't matter how much sadness I felt or how much I wanted to bury myself in a hole and never come out, dinner still had to be made. I wrote myself a check list, got out the potatoes, washed them, peeled them, chopped them and cooked them. Thawed the meat, cooked it in the pan. Then served dinner. I gave myself basic instructions to simply keep going. I didn't know what tomorrow would bring but I asked the universe to please let me wake up and find it had all been a bad dream. I was frightened to wake up and find the same reality. This thought made me lose sleep. Meditation worked to an extent – especially when I felt a warm feeling go through me and I knew I was really relaxed – but it wasn't long before I found myself wanting to scream at the top of my lungs, 'I want my old life back... I want Ben!' During the day, I used to head to a local beach and just sit looking out at the ocean and watching the sunset. I also started to think that maybe we needed to move house.

Ben's due date came and it was not as bad as I thought it was going to be. Amelia was at my parent's house so I didn't have to worry about being a wreck around her. It was very surreal and I didn't know what to do. I just wanted him back, I even bargained with God, 'Please, I will give an arm, leg and kidney to have Ben back.' I spent some time with girlfriends and that turned out to be fun. We spent four hours talking about anything and everything and I felt okay. That night

Kane and I received an invite to our friend's house for a drink. Well let's say it was not just one drink that was consumed, more like ten and I had a great time. The evening ended five hours later and I slept the night through courtesy of the vast amount of alcohol consumed.

Kane had so far been my rock and now I had to be his support. He had been getting more and more unwell. He was tired all the time. I found that after Ben dying, when one of us was low the other was okay. Given what we had been through it was not unexpected that he was unwell but he went for a check up anyway. I had heard it said that a major stress can exacerbate any underlying medical problem. He went for the usual blood tests and was called in to see the doctor again. His iron levels were extremely low and he needed to see a gastroenterologist to find out why. He got an appointment quite quickly and his doctor asked if he had suffered from any recent stress. Kane explained what had happened, but the doctor said nothing to him. Again, the unease that people felt and their inability to talk about death was coming through. Kane had a colonoscopy and was diagnosed with coeliac disease. We had to turn our eating habits completely around and everything now had to be gluten free. The diet change turned out to be a big distraction from our grief, and one of the biggest blessings in disguise was that we were unable to find any take away foods that were gluten free, so our eating habits improved tremendously.

In addition to improving our eating habits, I continued to exercise regularly. I did this for several reasons, to lose weight, to improve my chances of getting pregnant and to help improve my mood. I had group and personal training. My trainer was very understanding about the medical conditions and emotional experiences I had been through, and designed a program for me accordingly. Over a period of three months I was able to maintain a run on the treadmill and do a boxing session without feeling like I was going to die. I also enrolled in the university program for genetic counselling and was successful. When I look back, I realise that I managed to achieve many things that I did not think possible, yet I was oblivious to this at the time.

* * *

Amelia remained my source of inspiration to go on living; she was my reason for getting out of bed each day. The way she handled everything that was happening was amazing. We shielded her from a lot of things like going to hospital and the constant medical appointments but she showed me a side of managing grief that only a child can. One day I found her running around the kitchen and lounge room, and when I asked her what she was doing, she replied, 'Playing chasing with baby Ben.' I smiled and said, 'That's fine you can play.' A few moments later she ran to the front door, I asked why she stopped and she told me that baby Ben had flown out of the door and had gone off to do another activity. It was another precious moment that my children have given me.

* * *

Kane and I had contemplated selling our house several times over the past few years and had become friends with the real estate agent who sold us our home six years earlier. She happened to pop by one day to see how things were going. I told her that it was time to move on; I wanted to get out of the house because I was starting to feel like living there was a bad omen. On the other hand I didn't want to move because I had had all my pregnancies in the house and I felt comforted by this too. I was in a real state of confusion. We went ahead and completed the sale documents, but a day before it was to hit the market, we took it off. We just weren't ready to go. We had not found anywhere that was better than what we had. I had no energy to do the things that are essential for selling and buying like calling the bank, packing up the house, moving the dogs; but most of all I wasn't prepared to move away from the home in which we had our children. As much as there were aspects of our home we disliked, it had a special meaning for us. I was also concerned that people would look at Ben's things and I wasn't ready for that. I realised that it was not meant to be at that moment; other things need sorting first.

On many occasions I found myself sitting on our bed reflecting on my pregnancy with Ben. I recalled being so excited booking the ten-week appointment with my obstetrician as I had not made it that far in either pregnancy that had miscarried. I sat looking at Ben's scans and a print-out of his heartbeat. I was still working at the time and had been rostered a nightshift in the birthing suite. I was at twenty-weeks' gestation. I lay on a bed and placed the straps around my belly that recorded and traced his heart beat on paper. I listened and watched his heart beating away, daydreaming of what life would be like when he was born. Instead I was sitting on our bed looking at memories in a wooden box tied with a blue ribbon. At times I felt so sorry for myself but slowly I began to realise that I was not the only one in this situation. Looking through Ben's things reminded me of a talk I had been to about how women live in the developing world; where mothers leave their babies on the side of the road in the hope that someone will pick them up and give them a better life, when they were so starving themselves that there was no milk to feed their child. Giving up your baby because you cannot feed it even though you have the capacity to love it is a tragedy. I realised that these women grieve just as those in the developed world do, but thank goodness we have the necessities for life and access to great medical care. It made me appreciate what I had and where I lived and made me snap out of the 'why me' mode. I still had my uterus and could still have babies. There were other women in my position who had had hysterectomies and had not only had to grieve the loss of their child but also the fact that they could not have anymore.

Work continued as normal, or what my normal had become. I still found it difficult to answer questions that pregnant women would ask. In one situation I was attending a birth with my obstetrician and she changed the topic as soon as the woman asked how many children I had. I was grateful for these small things that made a big difference. Fortunately the women I was looking after all had normal births without complications and reminded me each shift that this was how it was meant to be.

part three
trying again

14

It was almost six months since Ben had died and my bad days had slowly started to become less frequent. I found that I had four or five bad days followed by two or three good ones. Losing a baby had become part of my reality and I found I couldn't imagine what I would be doing if Ben were alive. When this happened I felt enormously guilty just as guilty as when I had a day without him at the forefront of my mind. There was a noticeable difference between the initial shock and the way I felt at this stage. And sometimes I experienced all four emotions in one day. I was happy one moment then sad, guilty and angry the next. At the end of those days I felt fatigued and wanted someone to fix the pain, but knew that only time could do that. There were still times when I was driving the car when I wondered what would happen if I didn't turn the corner and just kept on going, but a picture of my family always appeared in my mind, and I realised that there was no way I would ever leave my daughter and husband. I also started to accept the finality of life, was not afraid to speak my mind and didn't care as much about what other people thought of me, as long as I was happy myself then that was all that mattered. I realised life was too short for games. I also had my first moment when I experienced real happiness. Amelia and I were playing in the backyard and I was pushing her on the swing when I realised that I wasn't faking my happiness. Until then I had followed my own mantra – fake it until you make it – and finally, I had made it. Well, just a little.

* * *

Kane and I had been given the all clear by our geneticist and obstetrician to start trying again for a baby. I was determined that this Christmas was going to be different. I got out my baby due date calculator and worked out which cycle I would need to fall pregnant in. Given we had always planned to try after six months, this worked out to be March. If we fell pregnant in March then the baby would be born in December. So we tried to fall pregnant. I was not a fan of trying to get pregnant, it absolutely did my head in, and in fact I think

I went a little crazy. For one half of the month my mood was fine and the second half, I was impatient to see if I was pregnant or not. It all had to do with being totally out of control. March was an especially difficult month for us. My sleeping was still all over the place and I seldom managed a full night's sleep. My anxiety was worse than ever because I had pinned my dreams on this month, the magic month. I prayed that the universe would grant me this gift after everything we had been through.

During the dreaded waiting stage Amelia celebrated her fourth birthday. As usual I went overboard wanting desperately for her to have a good time. She invited twenty-five friends to a children's play centre and she was the main attraction. Perfect. As I watched her I shed a tear; I was so proud of her and adored her so much. Amelia remained so full of life and love. She was well adjusted, happy and very innocent, even though she was only four years old. I hated how she had had to learn what death was at such a young age, but had gained knowledge that was so far beyond her years. I took some comfort in something a doctor told me – children in difficult situations do not feel the same pain as adults but what they feel is the sadness of watching their parents in pain, and only when they have children of their own will they fully understand what people go through. Hearing this brought such relief to me and I remembered my grandfather dying when I was a child. I didn't fully understand what was happening but I vividly recall my mum crying and being very sad. I can also recall what Pop had told Mum about life and death and that was, 'Life is for the living.' All these years later it became another mantra for me.

I was still attending counselling at SIDS and Kids and found that it helped me immensely. At each stage of my grief the counsellors were there. At each step I was reassured that my feelings were normal and the counselling helped me to come to terms with the possibility of losing another baby. I had to accept that just because I had had two miscarriages and lost one baby it did not mean it would not happen again. Each pregnancy had all the same risks attached. In addition to seeking help from SIDS I had a pre-pregnancy visit with my obstetrician to talk about the plan for another baby.

I longed to feel life in my arms again, a life filled with a healthy baby's cry and all the joys a child brings. This feeling was always accompanied with guilt and a sense of failing Ben because I knew that I could not give him life. The sense of failure extended to Kane and Amelia for not being able to give them a son and brother. I hoped that I could bring life back to our family once again through our new child, and that this would help me to be happy and be an active participant in family life again.

It was Ben's six month anniversary and my period was

due. This was the month I needed to fall pregnant to make my Christmas baby dream come true. I was devastated when the single line appeared in the pregnancy test stick window, followed by my regular period. It was a busy day with running Amelia around, going to work and by the end of the day I was a wreck. I was feeling an enormous sense of failure already but this just added to it. I couldn't believe it. Everything that I had hoped for came crashing down in a big pile and I felt devastated. This added to my sleeplessness and I found myself waking at midnight as well as 3am. I started to notice a pattern. Every time I woke up the clock said 12.22am. In the day if I looked at the computer it said 12.22pm and I even noticed the time on the oven, which is not set, said 12.22pm. It occurred to me when waking one night that that this was going to be my next baby's birthday. It felt right and there was a sense of calm attached to this feeling. It was an instant calm, almost like an awakening that everything was going to be okay. For once, it didn't take long to get back to sleep that night.

part four

tom

15

April came and Kane and I just went with the flow rather than trying for a baby. I didn't want to worry about the whole 'am I pregnant or aren't I' business again because it had done my head in the previous month – we actually missed the 'fertile' days by accident. This was how we fell pregnant with Amelia. Sure enough nature had similar plans and when I did the early pregnancy test (I couldn't help myself) there was a second pink line. I was thrilled. I was so excited and went to see my doctor immediately as I needed to go on to progesterone and Clexane once again. My baby was going to be born on December 22, just as the time on the clocks had told me.

When I got to the doctor's surgery I didn't quite get the same excited response that I had; more like, 'It's just a very faint line.' I just wanted someone to be as thrilled as I was. I had the blood tests taken and the results came back … positive! I was three weeks and five days pregnant! There was no denying!

I called my obstetrician's office to officially book an appointment. I didn't know who was more excited, the practice manager or me. She worked out my due date as 10th January 2009 and informed me that my obstetrician would be on leave that week. I reassured her that it would be a miracle for me to make a due date, as I had not made one yet; Amelia was born at thirty-eight weeks. I told her about my premonition and said as long as she is around on the 22nd December there would be no problem. We made all the scan and booking-in appointments and I felt relieved.

I realised very quickly that this was going to be a long pregnancy. As soon as the second line appeared on the test stick I finished work in the birthing suite. I realised that I couldn't possibly look after someone's pregnancy and baby while I had to focus on my own. I continued teaching the birthing classes but it wasn't long before I finished that too. My pregnancy was all consuming, so by ten weeks I had finished work. My baby was too treasured to put at risk and I simply couldn't live with myself if I did anything to contribute to a miscarriage. Right from the faint second pregnancy line I was in love.

My pregnancy care involved my obstetrician taking the regular blood tests that had previously been carried out at the fertility clinic and all of the scans. I felt so relieved to be in good hands and to have a single place to go to.

I went for my first scan at six weeks and saw the most beautiful sight I had seen in a long time, a little heart beating at 109 beats per minute and a tiny little dot measuring six millimetres. Yippee! I had jumped the first of many hurdles. For the next week I was so excited that I had managed to get pregnant again and have a baby with a strong heartbeat, and I booked in for the ten week visit.

It didn't take long for the excitement to wane. I hit week eight and I felt like I was ready to have the baby. The pregnancy was dragging already and I still had thirty weeks to go. Days started to feel like weeks and I found myself in a daze again, just going through the motions and only getting things half done. One morning I woke up startled. I had had a nightmare. In my dream I had gone for a scan at twenty-one weeks and my obstetrician couldn't see the baby. She organised surgery immediately to see what was happening and found a stillborn baby girl weighing 2100grams with curly brown hair. I woke up with an empty feeling in my stomach. I somehow managed to get Amelia ready for day care and then I hit the shops to try and distract myself by buying presents for children's birthday parties that Amelia had coming up. I bought all of them, wrapped them, did the cards and piled them into the present cupboard. That kept me busy until lunchtime but the thoughts about my nightmare had not subsided. I called my obstetrician's office and one hour later the girls had me in for a scan. The baby's heartbeat was a strong 174 beats a minute and the little dot had grown to twenty millimetres. We talked about all my fears associated with the pregnancy. She reassured me that fear and anxiety was going to be a part of the pregnancy and until the baby was crying in my arms I would be nervous. I felt much better for having someone who could put my emotions into words and understood this was a hard pregnancy. I headed home wanting to crawl into a burrow for the next six months but settled for a rest instead. I thought about the dreams I had and found a noticeable difference between my dreams that came true and those that didn't. When I had dreams that came true I did not feel anxious at all, I actually felt quite calm. I concluded from now on I would ignore the dreams that made me feel anxious and take note of the others.

Later that day I headed to SIDS and Kids for support and like always they were there for me. Everyone there celebrated my pregnancy. The mutual understanding we shared allowed us to know that each pregnancy was a blessing and even if this baby were to miscarry or be stillborn that he or she was loved and treasured. The counsellors allowed me to go through the rollercoaster of emotions and stood by me every step of the way; there was no right or wrong. I told them about my dream, how happy I was one moment and how crushed I felt the next and they explained that was okay, I was to expect that in this pregnancy and that only six months had passed since Ben had died. With my friend, I attended a group session on pregnancy following loss and it was very insightful and reassuring. I was comforted to know that I was among others who had similar feelings and even though all our circumstances were very different, our emotions were similar. It gave me the security to know I was doing okay, that it was still very early in my grief and I was not the only one. It was particularly important to know that there were others in similar positions because grief can be so isolating. There were days when I felt like the odd one out, like a statistic and at times some of my friends and colleagues did not know what to do or say. The people at SIDs and Kids were always there with a cup of tea and a hug, and my world was a better place because of the support they gave me.

16

Having finished work very early in my pregnancy I felt I was doing all I could to remain stress free. Well, as stress free as I could. I headed to my obstetrician's office for my first official pregnancy visit, the booking-in appointment. I was so excited to make it to this stage and actually have my piece of paper with all my details on it. It was a struggle when I got to the question about previous pregnancy as I did not know what to put about Ben; stillbirth, because that was what I thought it was, or neonatal death which was what Ben was classified as. I said neonatal death. It wasn't Ben's fault I didn't know he lived. I wanted to have him documented as he was and not to deny the 57 minutes he lived. It broke me all over again; it was the only time during the appointment that I cried. I couldn't bear the thought of him dying not in my arms; it physically hurt my heart and caused so much internal conflict and a longing to change things that were so far beyond my control.

* * *

My internal conflict reached the point where I was screaming in my head. Some days I felt like my head would explode. This was coupled with the enormous amount of guilt I felt because I didn't have the same feelings as when I was pregnant with Ben. I felt like my baby was okay, that it would live and be born on the 22nd December. All these emotions sent me into isolation. It was such an ugly stage and at the time I should have be talking to others and seeking help. Instead I stayed at home, in bed, crying, watching television and desperately trying to take myself so far away from where I was, but it didn't work. This was the insanity of losing a baby. Eventually I called my friend and realised that I was not the only one with these feelings, even though we lost our babies for very different reasons, our emotions were the same and we were in the same position. Later that afternoon, I got up again and went to collect Amelia from day care, and followed the routine motions again.

During times like this I would search the internet for something to give me some strength. One day I found a quote by an American journalist, Suzanne Pullen which said, 'The road I am on is my son's gift to me. The least I can do as his mother is to continue on this journey and see where it takes me.' This gave me hope and made me realise that everything in my life had Ben somewhere in it. I realised that even though he was not there he was always with me; sometimes I even felt him wrapped around me. I stopped taking so many things for granted and tried to live in the present. I threw my five year plan out the window and – inspired by a story I had seen on an episode of *Oprah* – replaced it with visualisations. Visualisations were more realistic to me and I created positive thoughts about what I wanted to achieve and then took action towards it. There were no specific time frames for achieving my dreams. My goals were flexible so I wouldn't feel like a failure if life took another hairpin turn.

Soon it was time for my twelve week scan, where my baby was to be screened for genetic disorders. I couldn't wait to see the heart beating again. It was the one ray of sunshine in this stage of my grief and pregnancy. The scan showed there was a strong healthy heartbeat of 161 beats per minute and the risk of the genetic disorders was oddly less than what Ben's were, even though I was older. To my surprise there were other reassuring features on this scan. The head, brain, heart, abdomen, tummy and bladder were all visible and appeared normal. I had not seen this on Ben's scan at the same stage of the pregnancy. The baby now measured just over six centimetres and I got my first look on the 3D scan. The pictures were lovely. I saw arms and legs and a little dot between them. I asked if it was a boy but there was no way of telling so early on. It was the first time I thought that this was probably going to be another boy and when I look back at the scans there was no denying it.

The rest of the day I spent asking myself why Ben couldn't have been as healthy and strong as this baby? Why did Ben have to die? Why does any baby or child? It is not 'right'. The order in life is not 'right'. Your children should out live you not the other way round. I reminded myself of what my grandfather said, 'Life is for the living.' It became my mantra again.

* * *

Part of my counselling was accepting that my baby could well be another boy. The first indication of this was when I headed back to the clairvoyant at six weeks' gestation and as soon as I walked through the door she looked at me and said I was pregnant with a boy. I had so badly wanted a girl so I wouldn't spend the rest of the baby boy's life comparing him to Ben and saying that's what Ben should be doing. I didn't want any confusion especially because Amelia kept saying that baby

Ben was back in my tummy. I spent hours with the counsellor talking about it, processing it and coming to an acceptance that it was beyond my control anyway. I was just happy to have a so far healthy pregnancy despite being on injections and suppositories every day. It wasn't long before I stopped the progesterone suppositories which I was very happy about. The needles gave me terrible bruising but it was all for a good cause, so I didn't care too much about that.

When I headed for my counselling session, I had time to look at all the pictures on the wall. The SIDS and Kids staff did an excellent job of displaying children's faces everywhere. All the pictures were of beautiful babies and happy infants and children and were an even mix of boys and girls. I had always seen them but never really looked at them before. For some reason I had always assumed that they were living babies and children born after the loss of a child, perhaps because when I worked in a fertility clinic the notice boards were filled with pictures of the 'success' stories. I looked at all the photos on the wall, and then took notice of the small print at the bottom. It was then I became aware that these were children who had died. I couldn't believe it, I was in shock and saddened that there were so many. It took me back to the dream I had had where a group of children were playing in a circle. The older children were on the outside supporting the younger children and babies. Ben was in the centre having a great time and laughing but even though the children parted so I could see Ben, no matter how far I reached, I couldn't get to him. It dawned on me that these other children in the park that day also had names and faces as I had seen on the wall at SIDS and Kids.

17

Amelia had pretty much had her own way for six months and now and it was starting to show. While Kane was around she would behave but when he was out at work she would play up. I had not had the energy to deal with discipline or establishing boundaries so I caved in every time she started playing up and just gave her what she wanted to keep the peace. Amelia had a knack of throwing tantrums in shopping centres. Before we had children I always said to myself our kids wouldn't do that – how wrong I was, in fact, I had one of the worse tantrum-throwers. At the age of two in an effort to get her own way she stripped off in the middle of Woolworths much to other shoppers' disgust, but I couldn't help but laugh as the tears poured down her face, she was quite a sight. This particular day, she had got her way already but her demands were getting quite ridiculous and after one cupcake I told her there were no more 'sometimes' foods. Well she threw a whopper right in the middle of the shopping centre. She started screaming, crying and demanding more. So with a trolley full of food I decided I had had enough and headed for the car. Realising this she lay on the floor holding the trolley. There I was, heading to the car pulling a four year old girl. It was quite a sight but I didn't find it as funny as I had before – after all, she was two years older than when she had done a similar thing before. Once we established our boundaries again we had a lovely day playing with her friends.

As I had started to show I was carrying a baby, Amelia decided that she would use my belly button as a microphone to the baby. She talked, sang songs, poked and kissed it all the time. It was the start of a very close bond between the siblings.

I was still questioning myself about how I would feel if I had another boy. I thought that I had had my boy and he was irreplaceable. I also knew that if it were another boy, it wasn't Ben. But would I love him as much? Would he die too? I was scared. Scared of losing another baby, scared of having another boy and scared of how I would feel when it was born. It also felt so surreal. The two months it took to get pregnant felt like years, and when I passed the first trimester I realised how close it was to the time I had lost Ben. My baby's due date was only two days away from Ben's due date. I had not thought of that before and realised planning to have a baby around the same time probably wasn't the best idea. Realising this made me even more fearful that I would constantly compare my new baby's life to what Ben's would have been like.

I leaned on the team at SIDS and Kids. One time when I dropped by there were two other mothers there and it was so reassuring talking to them; one of them had her baby the same day as Ben and was pregnant again as well. When we talked further about our situations we discovered we both had had chorioamnionitis but she was on prophylactic antibiotics. The difference between us was that she knew what type of bacteria had caused the chorioamnionitis and I didn't. I wondered why I was not on antibiotics as well. Up until now I had not realised that disposing of the swabs when Ben was born would have an impact on this pregnancy. I called my obstetrician and asked her about it. She said that because of this I would have to have vaginal swabs done each month of my pregnancy. I was even angrier that I didn't know what infection had killed Ben because it had an impact and threaten my pregnancy. Thankfully, the first set of swabs came back clear.

I was about to start university again and was really excited about getting some serious brain stimulation. Anticipating the start of the course gave me something else to focus on. My first subjects were bioethics and human reproductive biology, and I knew this would be a challenge on many levels.

I was having scans every other week and the results were all proving positive. The baby was growing and was at the 100 percentile for all growth parameters and my cervix remained long and closed. It was a relief. Life was more settled with me being at home occupied with studying, Amelia at day care and my worry about the pregnancy decreased. I found that I had started to accept that the pregnancy could be a boy. This was the first time that life was 'normal' in a long time; I was able to sit on my bed going through Ben's things without falling apart. I was very grateful for the break on the rollercoaster. It was coming up to Red Nose Day so my friend and I decided to volunteer for SIDS and Kids. It was the least we could do given all the help they had given us over the past months. We got into the swing of it and sold nearly everything they had given us that day, and we heard many stories of pregnancy loss from people our own age through to women in their later years.

Tax time was also fast approaching; I got our things ready for the accountant. I dislike tax time, other than when we get a good return, but this year was different. We had to declare Ben for tax purposes. I hated this. It was bad enough that we had a baby die without having to tell the accountant about it. It was awful for the accountant and for us. What was a good morning, turned into a bad day and I couldn't see why Kane and I had to be constantly reminded about our loss.

It seemed that everywhere I went women were pregnant or had babies, I felt like it was another slap in the face that Ben had died. This was not the same with my friends; I was thrilled to hear their baby news. At the same time, my emotions were in a state of flux. One minute I felt okay, the next angry. I was often asked by shopkeepers about the gap between the kids and depending on how much they pressed I would end up saying that I had had a baby die in between, and that soon stopped them talking. Amelia came out with some great stories. One shop keeper was told that baby Ben was given a poisoned apple and had gone to heaven. I wasn't there at the time, my mum was, and she called me to ask what I had been telling her. Amelia had made it up, based on the Snow White story.

On another occasion we were visiting a friend's baby in hospital and she was telling the volunteer in the play section that baby Ben had come down from the stars and was back in Mummy's tummy and would be born at Christmas. She said it with so much joy that I didn't bother explaining; others could make of it what they wanted. Amelia associated Ben with the stars and some nights we would sit there watching them together and some nights I would find her talking to the stars before she went to sleep. I was looking forward to knowing the sex so we could help her identify that this was a different baby.

Not knowing what killed Ben grated me constantly; I repeatedly asked my obstetrician about it and even asked if the results could have been filed under another name. There were people living in our area with similar names, I knew this because we had been mixed up before; once I even got a script with another lady's details on it by mistake. This was something that I continued to talk to the counsellor about at length. From talking to other people who have lost babies there always seemed to be one or two things that you have to accept that you can do nothing about. Mine were the missing test results and not knowing that Ben lived for 57 minutes.

* * *

I started to have a few contractions. They had come on and off the whole pregnancy, and it was diagnosed as an irritable uterus very early on. I was getting upset by them and one day my mum called and I just broke down. Mum organised a weekend of pampering and relaxation. It was just what I needed.

My obstetrician was going on holiday. I knew she needed a break as she seemed tired and cranky, maybe because I kept asking questions she couldn't answer, but when she went away I was absolutely terrified. The last time she went away I had had Ben. I had a scan and everything showed up as normal. The baby was growing well and my cervix was long and closed. I still couldn't find out the sex and had to wait another three weeks because the baby's legs were crossed. I was upset but I knew there was nothing I could do except sit tight and wait. All in good time I reminded myself, live for today.

Meanwhile, I spent considerable time studying. I was really enjoying it and it diverted attention away from my pregnancy and Ben. I was keeping up with the university recommendations, review questions and doing the assignments. It was a busy month, not only with university but catching up with friends as well. There was no time to have a baby before it was due!

There were several things that were different this month compared with the last. Firstly I didn't have what I called the PMT symptoms leading up to Ben's anniversary day, the third of each month. Normally I was fine from about the fifth of each month, then by the twentieth my mood started to change, leading up to my being upset, cranky and irritable when the third came round again. This particular month the third came and I forgot that it was Ben's anniversary completely. Not that I forgot about Ben but that Kane, Amelia and I had a lovely day at home and in our garden.

I actually enjoyed myself and didn't beat myself up for it. I was also starting to realise how strong I was to have lived through this and started to see some light at the end of the tunnel. I returned to work, I studied, had fun with my family and started to enjoy life again. I realised that my life was now divided into three stages, life before children, life after children and life after losing a child. I thought that there was nothing worse that could happen to me. I had experienced the lowest of lows that a woman could bear and yet I was still living. I felt like I was doing Ben proud. I also thought that he didn't want me to be sad. In all my dreams about him in the spirit world he was happy. I had only one dream in which he was resuscitated. Even then he only lived until sixteen months; in my dream he didn't grow to the size of a sixteen month old, he was constantly in and out of hospital and was on oxygen therapy all the time and he didn't sit, talk or walk and died in pain. This reassured me that his dying the day he was born was the right thing to happen. I wouldn't have wanted him to suffer.

***

Even though I wasn't working I was still getting reminders of the impact you have on women as a midwife. Amelia went to her dancing lessons as usual and a new mum was there.

She told me that I had looked after her when she came in with threatened premature labour and took the advice I gave her. In fact, she repeated back word for word what I had said. Her baby was born at thirty-eight weeks and was happy and healthy. She asked me how I knew it was a problem when she had called me on the phone: I replied that there were several symptoms of premature labour, back pain, odd cramping, feeling flushed, unwell and vomiting. Often it is a combination of these symptoms that indicate someone is going into premature labour and I always asked women who complained of these symptoms to come in to hospital for an assessment. She had seen the work-side of me and over time, learned about my personal passion behind the care that I gave.

Halfway through the pregnancy, I started to feel more relaxed. I even started enjoying it. People made comments that I was starting to 'glow' and the irritable uterus contractions I had experienced settled down. I had increased energy and was looking forward to decorating the baby's room as soon as we found out the sex. I could see our home and family coming together and felt more positive than I had done in quite some time.

Just as I had begun to settle and relax into the pregnancy, Amelia's day care called; there had been an outbreak of human parvovirus.

18

Parvovirus is not normally a problem except in pregnancy, in particular for women under twenty weeks' gestation. One expecting mum from the day care centre had tested positive and I called my obstetrician to ask about it. My concern was that prior to going on maternity leave I knew of a woman who had lost her second baby to this, which made me all too well aware that just because you have one stillbirth doesn't make you exempt from another. I went for a blood test my obstetrician had ordered and stopped by work to say hello. Well actually I kind of lost it and they ended up reassuring me and checking my baby's heartbeat; it was strong and healthy as usual. The girls at work were great, very understanding and supportive. They knew that while I was improving, it didn't take much to scratch my surface and get me worked up into a state of anxiety and panic about losing another baby. The blood tests came back clear.

* * *

The day of the big scan arrived, I was twenty weeks' pregnant and knew I could find out the baby's sex. My mother-in-law was visiting so we all went to see the baby. Given that I had pestered my obstetrician for the sex since my twelve week scan I thought I would say nothing and just let her tell me. About half way through nothing had been said so I asked, to which she said she knew the sex as soon as she put the scanner on! 'What! You're kidding!' I replied, 'I have only been asking about it my whole pregnancy!' Instead of telling me, she showed me. It was a boy. All my anxiety went out the window and all I felt was sheer joy and excitement. Kane was also excited, my mother-in-law was crying and Amelia said that she wanted a girl. To stir the pot I said, 'Don't worry, honey, Mummy can have another baby.' My obstetrician was gobsmacked and speechless, just the reaction I was looking for and we all started laughing. We had planned names for the baby from conception. Finally Thomas was here. Amelia now knew that it was baby Tom in Mummy's tummy and not baby Ben. Instead of just yelling at him through my belly button she started to sing the tune of *Number One Thomas* from the children's show. I truly felt like I had won a gold medal that day. Our precious and much longed for baby was happy and most importantly, healthy.

19

Tom was behaving himself and I was in a state of elation again. Given my seemingly happy disposition and new-found energy I tackled the kid's rooms. Not just the odd bit of tidying but two solid days of work. I didn't realise that I wasn't pacing myself and I woke at night with some contractions, not the usual irritable uterus contractions, and I had spotting as well. I took some of Kane's ventolin, as this can slow labour and some Panadol, and managed another four hours of restless sleep. In the morning I called the birthing suite and asked if they could see what my obstetrician wanted me to do as they were expecting her for the normal hospital round. One hour later I got a call to come in.

I dropped Amelia at day care and headed in. I didn't want to worry Kane so I decided I would call him when I knew more. Kane by chance called me and when he found out I was in the birthing suite he headed straight in, cranky that I had not told him what was happening. My obstetrician examined me and found that everything was reassuring but given my history I was to stay on bed rest at home and to take a drug three times a day to stop the contractions. I asked if I could still go on my weekend of pampering that my mum had organised, she didn't have to answer, as the look on her face said it all. I guessed that my thirty-fifth birthday party was also going to get canned. Oh well, I was pregnant for my thirtieth as well, but this was all for a good cause and I was happy to do as I was told.

I was in denial again and it took three days for me to realise that I was going to have another baby die if I didn't rest. That meant no vacuuming or hanging out washing, but I could take Amelia to day care. It was during times like these I noticed not having family close by. My mother-in-law arranged annual leave and spent five days with us and we arranged for house cleaning again. Friends helped us with meals and we arranged delivery of groceries on-line. All these things made life a little easier but also more expensive. It really wasn't an easy time… and it wasn't going to get easier.

The bi-weekly scans continued and were still very reassuring, Tom was growing safely inside me and although my resting had been hard on the family, I was actually starting to like pregnancy. I loved talking to him, rubbing my belly and having Amelia sing to him. It was such a wonderful change from the initial stages of pregnancy. I formed a bond with him even though there was still a little voice in the back of my head saying, 'Don't get too comfortable.'

One of my scans was scheduled for a late afternoon. I spent the day keeping Amelia occupied as any mum does with a four year old. We went to mothers' group, where I sat on a chair resting, then we did some light grocery shopping, returned home to cook dinner, then we went out again to visit a friend where I rested on her lounge. During the drive home I noticed I was having some contractions, actually I had been having them on and off all morning as usual so had not given them a second thought. Once I had dropped Amelia at home with Kane, I headed in for my routine scan.

Driving there I had a feeling I had overdone it that day. When I went in to see my obstetrician she said was happy with Tom's size of 992 grams but she still looked quite concerned. Technically I was supposed to be resting and most of the time I was, although the most difficult days were when Amelia was at home. When the results of the scan came back they revealed that my cervix, which up until now was long and closed, had started to shorten and what they call 'funnel'. It was opening from the inside. This with the contractions meant I had to be admitted to hospital. I pleaded to be able to stay at home but the situation was too serious given my history. I was only twenty-five weeks and two days pregnant. I headed home to break the news and I wasn't looking forward to it. Kane was perplexed and confused; together we wondered what we were going to do with Amelia and work. It was very stressful and to make matters worse I was having more contractions.

We got to hospital and as I walked through the door I saw a familiar face, one of my obstetrician's patients whom I had met when I was pregnant with Ben. I remembered her because we had talked about midwifery – she had gone through the training and I had encouraged her to come and work with us. As it turned out we had a similar history. I was so shocked and sad for her. She was wonderful and understood my position and helped me to a room and got me settled. Later I found out that she had also asked our obstetrician about me a few years ago, but as a practitioner you cannot discuss another patient so she did not know what had happened to me until now.

I was given more drugs to stop the contractions and injections to develop the lungs just in case Tom was going to be born. The drugs worked and the contractions settled. I was ordered bed rest with toilet privileges only and to stay on regular medication to stop labour. I really couldn't believe that Tom was going to be born, he wasn't supposed to come until the 22nd December which was twelve weeks away and somehow that gave me reassurance. That's not to say I wasn't filled with anxiety but part of me knew that it just wasn't time.

The next day I saw why I needed be in hospital to rest.

I simply had no possibility of resting fully at home. The first few days I actually enjoyed the break, no cooking, cleaning and washing. I felt like it was a bit of a holiday, watched all my favourite shows and got plenty of sleep except for being woken up at 3am to take my tablet to stop the contractions. After four days the novelty waned and I started getting very tired of looking at the same four walls. I also missed my family terribly. Kane and Amelia visited every day but it wasn't the same. Amelia was now at day care for four out of five days a week and Kane had to cut short his working day to drop her off and pick her up. Fortunately he had an understanding manager who gave him all the time he needed.

We tried to look at it like it was just a short period, but it was a long, long seven weeks. Kane set up the room with my computer and internet and I did home shopping for him but the days were still very long; once he had picked up Amelia and visited me, they wouldn't get home until 8pm which was a late night for Amelia and then they had to get up again at 6am to do the same thing. Some evenings I asked them to stay home if it looked like it was getting too much or they were really tired. Kane's birthday was coming up so I organised a gluten-free meal and cake, and we celebrated his birthday as a family in hospital with my parents. The next day was Ben's birthday. I was feeling very anxious about this day and didn't know what to do. I tried to record how I felt in a poem:

Midnight came and I was sleeping

I missed your visit at 3am

I prayed that you keep Tom safe.

I found your star Ben

It is the brightest in the sky

And I know you are shining down on us

I can't stop crying

Your dad is here

We cry together

So much relief that today is here

The anticipation was almost too much to bear

We share our time and open our hearts

I go through your things

And cry some more

Your sister and your baby brother are doing great

Dad goes

Time alone

Goodbyes whispered

Love for you and for life

You're always with us baby Ben

For eternity

Fly butterfly, fly

Life is for the living.

20

The following day I felt a weight lift off my shoulders, as if I had been set free. All the 'firsts' were complete. I had lived through the first Christmas, New Year, Easter and Ben's birthday and I was doing okay; I was more relaxed and calm. My hospital room was starting to look like home. I had my scan pictures of Tom on the wall and a good friend had taken pictures of Amelia and blown them up so I had posters of her around the room as well. Up in the corner I had Ben's box so I could go through his things if I wanted. The computer was now set up as a DVD player to so I could watch *Law and Order* whenever I wanted. People had brought in books, magazines and movies so that I wouldn't get so bored.

One week into my stay I noticed that I was having some loss again. I was twenty-six weeks' pregnant. I did the same thing as when I was pregnant with Ben and took some swabs. The results were positive indicating that I had possibly ruptured the membranes around my baby again. The staff rushed me to the birthing suite where the weekend obstetrician examined me and carried out some further tests. Thankfully, all the results were negative; Tom was safe for another day. I measured my pregnancy day-by-day and hoped I would make it to twenty-eight weeks. I knew there was a 95 percent chance Tom would survive if I made it till then.

I was going slightly crazy on bed rest, but watching *Oprah* always had a way of making me appreciate what I had. There was an episode on dying and acceptance of death. I watched a man speak from his heart to his children in what were to be the last months of his life. The message echoed that the biggest regrets a person could have were for the things he or she didn't do. I knew if I didn't rest it would be my biggest regret. If I did not rest Tom would be born early.

My studying kept me busy and I completed a subject from my bed. The other subject was not as easy and I couldn't sit the exam, so I had to defer it. The other thing that I did was shop. I discovered internet shopping and I had the time to search for the best prices. It was great 'nesting' and while I couldn't do it at home I gave it a good shot from the hospital. I discovered all sorts of things; I purchased a new style of hemp and bamboo nappies, clothing, nappy bags and a beautiful pale blue muslin sling, which was my favourite. The postman became very familiar with my address. After buying my sling I slowed down the spending because Kane and Amelia had to eat! There was one thing I couldn't resist. I was missing Amelia terribly. She was my ray of sunshine in the world and so I ordered a box of flowers with a balloon and teddy online and arranged for it to be delivered to her at day care. She loved it; she was the talk of the school for the day.

* * *

This pregnancy felt different. I could feel that Tom was strong and I could feel his movements all the time. The bed rest gave me so much time to bond with him. When Amelia came in for visits, she sat with me and talked and sang to Tom. At the weekends Kane dropped her off for some quality 'mum time' and we coloured, drew pictures, played Barbies and watched movies. The midwives were great and took good care of her. She got to know them all by name and started helping herself to the biscuits in the kitchen. Leaving was always hard but it meant a trip in the lift. We had a routine of waving to each other from the hospital room window to the car park. Each time Amelia left we would blow kisses and sign 'I love you' to each other. She was doing great considering the circumstances. Kane was feeling the effect of having me away. It was taking its toll, and he was so worried we would lose Tom too. He was doing great managing Amelia and that was all that mattered.

I had so much time on my hands I could daydream all I liked. I actually started to think I may take this baby home. What would it be like this time? What was I going to do? I almost felt a little out of place in the world. It was as if I had come to a point where I expected to lose another baby. I spent hours talking to my friends about how unusual it was going to be to not have to grieve for this baby, wondering what to expect having another baby live, would I love him the same amount as my other children? The midwives would sometimes sit with me for a couple of hours after a shift letting me talk through all the clutter in my head so I could process it. During this time I found some true, invaluable friends.

Financially the budget was tight and I didn't want my parents to continually help us out of tricky situations, so I did some investigation into our insurance policies. I realised why I had been paying insurance premiums for so many years. The insurance covered a private hospital room with my own bathroom, TV including Foxtel, full home-style cooked meals and I was seen every day by a well-respected obstetrician who specialised in foetal medicine!

Kane and I had taken out life and income protection insurance when we purchased our first property. We were only in our mid-twenties at the time but we had watched one of our friends go through the heartache of losing her husband just months after their wedding. It was heartbreaking. She didn't expect the vow 'until death do us part' to happen so soon. Kane and I learned from this and made sure that if that were to happen to us, financial issues wouldn't be a part of grieving. Ten years on we were still paying into our income protection policy. I investigated if the policy would cover me in my situation and it did. In total the insurance company paid us quite a substantial amount of money. We were able to repay my parents money we had borrowed and any related bills, day care fees, cleaners and food were covered for the remainder of the pregnancy. What we had contributed over the years was paid back to us. I was so glad we had never stopped paying into our insurance fund, even when money had been tight.

21

The twenty-eighth week of my pregnancy finally arrived. I had done it. I had achieved the first milestone. If Tom was born early he had a good chance of survival. It was also time for my gestational diabetes screening test. It was bittersweet because I hadn't made it this far with Ben. I hated this test. I had to drink so much sugar I felt like vomiting. The results came back and were positive indicating that I had gestational diabetes. I needed to have another diagnostic test, which meant consuming an even greater amount of sugar. It was horrible. The result of this test was borderline negative but because of my pregnancy history and the size of Tom, it meant that I was treated as a gestational diabetic. I had an appointment with an endocrinologist and then commenced testing my blood sugar levels four times a day. As I wasn't allowed out of hospital, I had phone consultations and I was put on a gestational diabetic diet. For the first few days my blood sugar levels were okay, but then started to creep up.

My dietician and endocrinologist were very strict with the levels so even a minor change above normal meant action. I started on a drug called Metformin that was approved for use in pregnancy. My levels were normal for two weeks and then started to creep up again. In a way this saved me from insanity. I was going crazy looking at the four walls of my room, so occasionally I went for a walk to the staff desk or kitchen just for a change of scenery. I always did it when my obstetrician wasn't around but she always found out and I was always in trouble. My sugar levels continued to rise, which meant I had to go on insulin. Although it meant being jabbed with a needle every day, it also meant I could leave the hospital to go to my endocrinologist's room. I was so thrilled to see daylight and breathe fresh air.

During one of my trips to the staff desk I realised how big Tom was growing. The desk was ten paces away from my room, so in the quiet times I wandered out and talked to the staff. On one occasion a visitor was looking for her friend and commented that I looked due any day. When I replied that I wasn't she then asked me if I was having twins!

The upside to being in hospital, especially with gestational diabetes, was that I hadn't gained any weight. Sure, Tom was gaining weight himself, but mine remained stable as all the meals were calorie-controlled. I was very happy about that as I had struggled to lose weight after my previous pregnancies.

In hospital I watched so much *Law and Order* I thought Tom was going to recognise the gongs on the show before he recognised me, and I knew he was going to love Oprah, because he constantly heard her voice. One *Oprah* episode inspired me to create a vision board of how I wanted my life to be. I got all my magazines and cut out pictures, headlines and stories and made a collage in a large notebook. I wrote down things that were important to me at the top of each page: life; family; health; home; dreams and aspirations, and filled each page with pictures and sayings I found comforting and inspiring. Looking at my vision board reassured me that I could move forward and achieve positive things even when life at times seemed unjust, unfair and difficult.

22

It was soon time for my obstetrician to go on holidays and I hit panic mode that Tom was going to arrive. She assured me that she would come into the hospital if I went into labour during the first half of her break; otherwise I would have to have the on-call obstetrician. I kept reading the sayings on my vision board and didn't move from the bed the whole time. I did not want Tom to be born early.

Having made it to thirty weeks into my pregnancy my next goal was thirty-four. The scans showed things were improving and my cervix was going back to normal. My obstetrician said I could go to the coffee shop and back and I was thrilled with the welcome escape from my room. She even said I could possibly go home earlier than expected. If I made it to thirty-four weeks, baby Tom could be born at the hospital I was already in. Any earlier he would have to be born at the tertiary public hospital where Ben had been born and I really didn't want to go back there.

The next couple of weeks were busy. I had assignments due and my friends had organised a baby shower for me in hospital. They were fantastic and did everything from getting the cake to organising games and decorations. In the lead up to my baby shower I finished an assignment and, given my additional privileges, I walked to my obstetrician's rooms to return a bioethics book she had leant me. She was horrified that I had walked so far, even though it was only across a car park and back. I quickly gave her the book and headed back. I hoped it didn't mean I had to stay in my room all the time. Thankfully it didn't and I was allowed to wander to the lift to say goodbye to Amelia and Kane at the end of their visits. That week my mother-in-law came to stay and help out, which was great. She sorted all the washing, including all the things I had for baby Tom, and she helped Kane with the cooking. We were so grateful for all her help. One of the members of staff from SIDS and Kids also came to visit me. I was so happy to see her again. She had made several calls and sent me text messages while I was in hospital, but to see her was fantastic. She was a lifeline in my troubled times.

The day of my baby shower arrived and all my friends came. It was wonderful to see everyone again. The day was faultless and my friends had done a perfect job. The cake was in the shape of a baby with a blue nappy; it was fantastic. We all had a drink and something to eat and I opened all the lovely presents. A wonderful day was had by all. I needed a drop of extra insulin that night as I broke the diabetic diet for the cake. It was all for a good cause.

I was quite used to all the finger pricks and needles by now. I was even able to adjust the amount of insulin I was taking, as I knew the parameters which the endocrinologist and diabetes educator worked within. The amount of insulin I required was slowly increasing as the pregnancy was progressing but that was normal. It was a good thing that I was treated as a diabetic as Tom was on the 100 percentile for growth. I wondered how big he would have been if I didn't go onto insulin and the diabetes educator reminded me that untreated mothers have babies usually born at thirty-five weeks that weigh the same as a full term baby. These babies have to go straight into the special care nursery with drips and on oxygen. It had been ten years since I had seen this. One particular baby I remember was born at thirty six weeks and weighed 4.5 kilos and the head box to deliver the oxygen only just fitted. After recalling this I felt even better about doing the insulin injections.

I always looked forward to scan days as it meant another picture to add to my wall. My room looked very homely and I had settled down somewhat. I was last on the list of appointments for one of my scans. Kane wheeled me over to my obstetrician's consulting rooms in a wheelchair, as I was still not allowed to walk across the car park. The scan showed my cervix remained long and closed and Tom was a growing on the same 100 percentile. Out of the blue my obstetrician gave me the best news… I was allowed to go home! Whooohooo! I was out, but only on the condition that I did nothing other than take Amelia to and from day care. Then she realised I was only thirty-one weeks' pregnant and hesitated. I insisted I would be okay as my mother-in-law was coming down again to help for the week. I was allowed to go! I was so excited by the news and went back to my room to pack up. I filled the four-wheel drive to the top with all my things. I couldn't wait to see Amelia again.

23

Seeing Amelia again gave me so much joy. She was surprised, excited and a little confused at the same time. Each doctor's visit I attended she would ask if I was coming home. It broke my heart and I realised how much my stay in hospital had affected her. Walking through my front door, I could tell Kane had not expected to be taking me home after the scan – the place was a disaster zone! Oh well, I didn't care. I was home and he tidied up while I sat with Amelia. I organised the cleaner and my mother-in-law came and helped with the washing while I sat on the lounge folding the freshly-washed clothes. I felt hopeless as I wasn't able to do the things I normally did. But it was either this or back to hospital. Rest it was.

Three weeks passed by and I finally hit the thirty-four

week mark and celebrated! The scan from this time showed that Tom weighed three and a half kilos. He was the size of a full term baby; actually he was the size of Amelia when she was born. It was no wonder I couldn't breathe and my ribs were constantly sore. Despite this, I was given permission to come off bed rest and just take things easy. My obstetrician and I talked about the way Tom would be born. Given his size, if I were to have a vaginal birth I would have to go into preterm labour, otherwise a date would be set for a caesarean section in the coming weeks. Great. After trying not to have the baby, I now had to try and give birth in the next few weeks.

* * *

It was a Sunday evening and I was attending to Amelia while sorting out dinner and I had the news on the TV in the background. It wasn't the normal station we watched but I was too busy with Amelia to change the channel. I overheard the news reporter talking about a little boy who had died in an accident and the name sounded familiar. I stopped and looked up to see a picture one of my good friends with her son. It was one of the mums from Amelia's dance group. I had watched her son grow up from when he was a newborn. I froze. I was in shock. I got my out mobile and sent her a text message thinking the newsreader had made a mistake. There was no mistake. I was so very sad for her. It was going to be a hard road ahead and I hoped I could support her just as she had supported me after Ben's death. The thought of him dying was incomprehensible. The cute little boy who we saw go from sitting to standing to walking; and his beautiful happy face. Life is so cruel.

My friend's little boy's funeral was held at the same venue as Ben's. I had not been back there since Ben's funeral so a friend came with me to provide support. I was immediately struck by the surrounds again – a beautiful sunny day with the green rolling hills, ponds and birdlife. The funeral was attended by hundreds of people and my friend did her son proud. She had the strength to deliver the eulogy and it was a wonderful tribute to his little life. It broke my heart and I stood there crying. I knew she would say the final goodbye after the mourners had left. It reminded me of my final goodbye with Ben. We all went outside and my friend's family released balloons. There was not a dry eye to be seen.

* * *

The following week I did all the essentials to prepare for baby Tom's arrival. I got the car seat fitted and had an appointment with the diabetes educator. My insulin intake had been increasing as the pregnancy progressed, as expected. Amelia had a weekend away camping with friends and their kids. She had a great time and Kane and I got to spend some time alone together. I was approaching the thirty-fifth week of pregnancy, so I decided to put all the natural inductions of labour to the test. If I was to have a natural birth then I had two weeks to do it. I tried everything: sex, curry, sex after curry but nothing happened. I couldn't believe it! I had just spent seven weeks in hospital trying to stop labour and now I couldn't bring it on. Typical! I spent the week doing everything I wasn't supposed to be doing. I ran about and finished decorating Tom's room, took Amelia for play dates, attended more doctors' appointments and even went to a Christmas party but still nothing happened.

At my next obstetrician's appointment it was decided that as Tom was so big – he measured forty-three centimetres at thirty-six weeks – I would have a caesarean section on, Monday December 22. It was just as the clocks had predicted nine months earlier.

I spent the week leading up to the birth finishing off wrapping Christmas presents and getting the final baby bits organised. I couldn't believe that next week I would have a baby, a baby to take home. I had one final appointment with the diabetes educator to discuss the insulin I would need before the birth. As a final precaution I was having more steroid injections to mature baby Tom's lungs, and one of the side effects was an increase in my blood sugar. So the insulin dose was altered and I was ready.

24

I was admitted to hospital the night before Tom's birth to keep an eye on my blood sugar. Fortunately my sugar levels were the best they had been in a while and I didn't need any additional insulin. I was full of apprehension and excitement and sleep was the last thing on my mind. Christmas Day was in three days' time and I was getting the best present of all. I unpacked my things and settled in for the night. I spent extra time paying attention to Tom's movements as this was the last time I could feel him kicking and punching. It was also, perhaps, the final time I would be pregnant so I wanted to make the most of this quiet time. Kane went home and Amelia went to stay with my parents. All was good. As I was about to turn off the light the phone rang. It was my friend who had lost her son in the accident. I desperately wanted to see her. I wanted to take her pain away. I talked to her as she had done with me one year earlier and listened to what she had to say. I knew she would live through her pain. She was strong, a survivor. When the anger, despair and sadness started healing she would see the light at the end of the tunnel.

I woke early on the morning of the 22nd December. In the birthing suite after Ben was born, Kane and I had planned a pregnancy for six months time and a baby just before Christmas. Ben was taking good care of me and our family. I showered and dressed for the theatre with the thrilling thought of having my baby in my arms in a matter of hours. Kane arrived with the same anxiety and excitement of meeting our second little boy. Between us we babbled and fussed over cameras and clothes, and planned for the coming few days. I took an angel coin a friend had given me and Ben's hat to the operating theatre to give me strength. The midwife came to see me and then it was time to go. My heart was racing as I lay in the bed. The bed rails were pulled up, the brakes taken off and I was wheeled along the corridor to the operating theatre. I felt like a child waiting to see Santa. I had been waiting for three years and it was my turn. I was pushed into the operating theatre, where the anaesthetist inserted a drip into my arm. I was sitting while the anaesthetist inserted the epidural into my spine and I lay down. I was busy talking to him and Kane and a few moments later I asked the anaesthetist if he had put the catheter in. He told me that the catheter had already been inserted and my skin had been cut. I couldn't believe it. I was shocked, not because I had expected to feel anything, but because time was moving so fast.

It seemed like only a few minutes later the theatre staff dropped the screen and Kane and I saw the most beautiful sight, a big baby boy. He was just beautiful and the moment I laid eyes on him I knew he was always meant to be here. All my fears and anxiety disappeared. This time Kane and I shed tears of joy instead of pain. They wrapped Tom and gave him to us. I was in awe. I just adored him. I was totally in love, so much so that the paediatrician had to pry him out of my arms to give him oxygen. When I look back at the photos I see why, he was purple but at the time I didn't notice. I only saw the most beautiful and healthy baby. His colour came good and he didn't leave my arms except to be weighed and measured. He didn't need special care either. The staff did the routine baby care while I was in theatre and at thirty-seven weeks and two days he weighed just over four kilos! With the stitching complete I was transferred into recovery where he attempted his first breastfeed. The little trooper even had a few sucks. Due to the gestational diabetes he needed his blood sugar monitored. It was not unusual for these babies to need some special care, but my Tom held his own and the first blood sugar level test was good. To stop it dropping I gave him top-ups of formula milk so that he didn't have to be taken away from me and spend time in the special care nursery. Sure enough his sugar levels remained fine and he fed as well on my breast as he did on the bottle.

I was transferred back to my room and I started using the pain relief right away. I knew that if I didn't then I would end up playing a game of catch up and be in too much pain to manage my Tom. Before Amelia and the family arrived I dressed Tom in all the clothes I had got for him during my hospital stay. He looked so cute. He had big chubby cheeks and the biggest eyes I have seen on a baby. I couldn't leave him alone. I got the first pictures up onto Facebook by lunchtime. That's how excited I was to show him off. I was looking forward to seeing Amelia and for her to see Tom. She had talked and sung to him the whole pregnancy and she loved him immediately. He went as easily to her for cuddles as he did to me. It was immediately apparent that they had a special bond that would last their lifetime. My parents were besotted with him too. It was a lovely day and with only family visiting it gave me the chance to spend lots of time with him. I had been worried about how I would feel toward Tom when he was born, but all the worry disappeared when I first saw him. He was different to Ben, although in his sleep his facial features were very similar. That evening, aided by the pain relief medication, I was able to get out of bed. It was recommended that I tried to get up in the first twelve hours after the caesarean. I was not able to sleep very much with the state of awe I was in. In the first twelve hours of Tom's life we had already taken about one hundred photos and dressed him in several outfits. I eventually got some rest. Again the sounds of *Law and Order* put me to sleep but now for a different reason.

I woke quite early the next morning and the midwife on the night shift helped me to the shower. By the time my obstetrician came in I was up and dressed! I laughed with her that I could do it again tomorrow. It was like all the worry had vanished the moment I saw Tom and I had completely forgotten about the stress of the last nine months. I'm sure she was hoping that I was joking. I don't know if either of us could go through it again. Everything had gone to plan with the caesarean and Tom was doing well. It was unusual to have things go to plan. Breastfeeding was going much better this time around. With Amelia I had had a lot of trouble and had had to use nipple shields and express milk and bottle feed top-ups. Tom seemed to go well with the feeding and he went straight on to the breast. No fussing, just sucking properly. There was no pain and he was settled after a feed. I had come to hospital prepared with nipple shields and bottles. It is amazing that the experiences were so different between

Amelia and Tom, but so were their births. Amelia was born after twenty-two hours of hard labour and a vacuum delivery. I could barely walk to the shower after she was born and had to stay in hospital for six days. Tom was planned and much less traumatic and the milk seemed to flow more easily.

The day before Christmas Eve was busy. I had lots of visitors and it was good to see everyone and show Tom off. By the end of the day I was exhausted but made myself walk down the corridor and back. I still didn't feel any pain as I was taking medication very regularly. Sleep was disrupted with the cries of hunger, but it was music to my ears. I fed him and he went back to sleep, but not before I gave him plenty of loving looks and whispered sweetly in his ears. This early form of communication is vital yet so often missed. Babies recognise the voices they became familiar with in the womb. Tom recognised Amelia's voice before Kane's as she was always using my belly button as a microphone. After feeding Tom would settle close to me for a while before I put him back into his crib where he would carry on sleeping.

The next day when my obstetrician came to check on me I asked if I could go home. There was no real need for me to stay in hospital as I could take the pain killers at home. I was also able to use the bathroom sink to bathe Tom in without bending, which was forbidden after my operation. I had spent far too much time in hospital; I wanted to go home. I was given the all clear and Tom was seen by the paediatrician who was happy with him too. The midwives took good care in giving me everything I needed for a peaceful few days.

With a feed under our belt we headed out. How lovely it was to take him home. I was completely overjoyed. There were no day three blues, which new mothers often experience as their hormone levels start to change after having a baby. Actually, there were no blues at all. I was just so happy and so in love with Tom. Once at home I put him in his bassinette next to our bed and he slept. Amelia came home from my parents where she had been staying and this year on Christmas Eve we had peace in our home.

* * *

Christmas morning came and Santa had been. Santa had many surprises this year; he had been to Disneyland on-line and had bought princesses and cars galore. I gave Amelia and Tom a present from Ben. It was such a special, yet chaotic, morning with the four of us. We brought Ben's candle out and lit it in his memory, I even sat his ashes on the television unit for the day. We all experienced a new set of firsts; the first Christmas with our family complete although one was missing. I had the best Christmas present of all, Tom. There was no greater gift. He was a miracle and a gift from the angels. There was no topping this Christmas.

Lunch time approached and as we had done the year before we headed to the same restaurant with my parents. This year instead of grief there was joy. Tom slept under the table the whole time. We ate a traditional Christmas lunch and when sufficiently full, headed home as a family.

Amelia spent some quality time with my parents during the following week, while Kane and I were settling in with Tom. For a change in our home, life was calm. Tom fed well and slept well, and had the occasional play in between. He loved his baths and massages but most of all his cuddles. We need not have run around organising rooms as Tom slept in mine and Kane's room. Now there was myself, Amelia and Tom in the one room, while Kane still slept in Amelia's princess bed. It was what worked in our house. Tom was a snugly boy just like his sister and we had no trouble obliging him.

The New Year came and we celebrated with friends. I even stayed up for the midnight fireworks and thought how my life had changed in such a short period of time. I now had two sons. I looked to the stars and gave thanks for the blessings in my life, especially for what my children had shown me. Amelia showed me that you can have it all just not all at once; Ben showed me that the love between a mother and child lasts an eternity and had no bounds; Tom showed me the absolute joy motherhood brings.

25

Tom was an extension of our family. He just fitted in right from the start – he had to as life continued on. Amelia was starting school at the end of the month and we had many preparations ahead. We also had a trip to Kane's family planned. Two weeks after Tom was born we headed north for another family celebration of Tom's birth and Amelia's going to school. The last time I went to my in-laws' house was when I was twenty-weeks' pregnant with Ben and I can recall vividly saying to my father-in-law that the next time we would be here we would have another baby. True to my word that was the case, just with a different son.

We returned home after a lovely week of celebrations and we started to get ready for the school year. I had already sewn up the hems of Amelia's school uniforms and all I needed to buy were socks. Santa had given her a bag and matching lunch tote with a picture of her favourite Disney character on the front, Ariel the mermaid. My parents visited again and we recorded the day with some lovely photos of Amelia and Tom. I was so proud of Amelia for the journey she had been on, how she had managed to accept what had happened to Ben and how happy she was with her brother Tom.

We celebrated Australia Day with our closest friends. Over the years we had shared many lunches and dinners together so Kane and I felt it was fitting to share the champagne we bought fourteen months earlier when I was having treatment at St Vincent's Hospital. With kids crying, laughing and playing around us we toasted the safe arrival of Tom and the news that one of our friends was pregnant. The moment could not have been more appropriate. We finished our celebrations and headed home. That night Kane and I sat outside looking up at the stars. Silently I shed a tear for Ben and although I still missed him every day our family had started to move on in happiness, healing and appreciation for what we had.

afterword

Being stuck in hospital helped me learn a valuable lesson; if I was not happy and feared the future, then the grass was always going to appear greener on the other side. I realised I had the choice to either remain scared of what the future held, or enjoy the moment and appreciate all its value. I knew I had to start appreciating what I had. Looking back, it was clear to see how my career affected my life. I had taken a five year break from hands-on midwifery whilst I worked for a pharmaceutical company. I loved it at the time and while I had no children it was great. I travelled the country and enjoyed the pressure of the job, but when I had Amelia I realised that it wasn't going to work. I stopped enjoying the travel and the long hours and the pressure interfered in my relationship with Amelia. But it was only after my first miscarriage that I realised I would have to leave the position. I had not resigned earlier because I was so scared of not knowing what was out there. It was only when I went back to midwifery that I realised that this was what I loved. It didn't feel like work. I had the flexibility of shift work; life was balanced and with Amelia in day care, less it meant the bills could still be paid even though my income had dropped. I now know I will never stay in a job I am not satisfied with again, and as the saying goes, love what you do and you will never work a day in your life.

Life was returning to normal. My emotional highs and lows were becoming less frequent and instead of bad days there were only bad moments. The shoes of grief were becoming easier to walk in. Amelia started school without any hiccups. Tom was doing everything a baby should and my recovery was going well. Having Tom was actually more healing than I expected, and the joy that he brought to our family was irreplaceable.

I saw the clairvoyant not long after I had Tom and she reminded me that he truly was a miracle. She also told me that Ben is proud of how our lives have continued and wants only happiness for us. I found great comfort and relief in her readings and words.

Ben's urn sits on my bedside table alongside photographs of Amelia and Tom on their christening days. Kane's and my bedroom is surrounded with angel remembrance gifts, which give me comfort and reassurance. We continue to remember Ben each and every day. For his anniversary we spent some time away. I wanted to make sure we did something happy as a family because I'm sure Ben wants us to live life like that.

Before having Ben I didn't have any friends who had lost babies or children, and now I have quite a few. In fact now I now volunteer for SIDS and Kids and fundraise for them each year, and through this I have made lots of friends who have had similar experiences to my own. Volunteering gives me the satisfaction of knowing I am giving something back to those people who helped me through the darkest of times. Those who are closest to me have all gone on to have another child and all boys too. Their friendship continues and I hope that I have helped and supported them as much as they have me.

Writing this book gave me the chance to honour Ben. It was my outlet for expressing my deepest feelings and emotions that I just couldn't speak about. Looking back it amazes me how healing I found writing, and I can see how far I have come through the grieving process. Writing even made me recall a few things I had forgotten about Tom's pregnancy and it made me appreciate more than ever how fortunate I am to have him. I hope that other people in a similar situation are able to find strength from my family's experiences. Initially the last thing you want to hear is that time heals but that's how life works. It is a journey of discovery and learning about yourself and others. I now feel like I can face anything head on as I have lived through one of the worst experiences possible. The echoes of my grandfather's words continue to ring, 'Life is for the living'. And even though life is a rollercoaster, I have started to appreciate the ups so much more for going through the downs.

acknowledgements

Kane, we make a good team in life – I love you.

To Milly and Tom, my little bumble bees – you are the reason I get up every day, I love you every second, every minute, every hour, every day.

Our families, Mum, Roland, Anne, Lindsay, Mat, Kaori, Corinne, Beth, Pete, Jane and Geoff.

Thank you to the obstetric and neonatology teams from Newcastle's Private and Public Hospital. Special thanks to Dr Jillian Spilsbury and her staff for six years of continual expert care, understanding, and patience. To Dr Andrew Pesce at Westmead Hospital and the interventional radiology team at

St Vincent's Hospital for all their assistance, proficient care and sense of humour. With your help we have our beautiful children.

To the midwives who assisted us on Ben's birthday – Chris, Meagan, Sally, Faye, Marilyn, Jenny and Fiona.

A very special thank you to all the team at Hunter SIDS and Kids, in particular, Sue-Ellen, Phil, Robyn and Shelly.

Chris Budden for all you have done for our family, we are so grateful.

Jackie – you are my link to the stars.

To our places of work for their continual understanding in what was the most difficult of times.

There are many friends to thank – Sueanne, Lucas, Chad, Tracy, Ed, Tanya, Alison, Grant, Maurice, Jenny, Paula, James, Dea, Faye, Sue D and Sue W, Leonie, Mel D, Michelle, Jane, Jayne, Carly, Georgina, Debbie, Vanessa, Nataria, Mel V, Sarah and school mums – I will always be grateful for your friendship and thank you for listening day in and day out throughout this journey.

Brooke, Kate, Jen – there are no words, you know how I feel.

To the photographers: Deb for giving us such beautiful pictures during my pregnancy; Carly for writing Ben's name in the sand and all your precious photos; Kelly for making a dream come true and for giving me photos of our three children together and for giving Ben the moon and stars.

Finally, to Jane Curry Publishing for taking a chance on me and Caroline for having an instant understanding – the only words that come to mind are, 'You get it'. Thank you.

Organisations that may be able to help

SIDS and Kids
Phone: 1300 308307
Web: www.sidsandkids.org

SANDS Australia (Stillbirth and neonatal death support)
Phone: 1800 228655
Web: www.sands.org.au

Stillbirth Foundation Australia
Phone: 02 9967 3229
Web: www.stillbirthfoundation.org.au

Bonnie Babes Foundation
Phone: 1300 266643
Web: www.bbf.org.au

Teddy Love Club – Parent and Infant Loss Support
Phone: 1800 824240
Web: www.teddyloveclub.org.au

To Write Their Names in the Sand
Web: www.namesinthesand.net